PERSISTENT RESISTANCE

*Calls for Justice from
the Celtic Traditions*

PERSISTENT RESISTANCE

Calls for Justice from the Celtic Traditions

A Collection of Essays

Ellyn Sanna, Editor

Copyright © 2019 by Anamchara Books, a division of Harding House Publishing Service, Inc. The original essays in this book may not be reproduced or transmitted in any form or by any means, electronic or mechanical, including photocopying, recording, taping, or any information storage and retrieval system, without permission from the publisher.

The quotations in this book are taken from the speeches and writings of historical and present-day activists and have been changed only to allow for gender-inclusive language. Quotations from the Bible are the editor's own paraphrases from the Hebrew and Greek, unless otherwise noted.

Page and cover design by Micaela Grace.
Ilustrations by Jeffrey Thompson (www.karmadogs.com/jef).

Printed in the United States of America.

Vestal, NY 13850

www.anamcharabooks.com

IngramSpark 2020 ISBN:
978-1-62524-810-7

How wonderful it is that nobody need wait a single
moment before starting to improve the world.
Anne Frank

Dripping water hollows out stone,
not through force but through persistence.
Ovid

> The world is waiting
> to hear from you.
>
> —Leymah Gbowee

CONTENTS

How to Read This Book	11
Introduction *Ellyn Sanna*	19
1. What Is Justice? *Marjorie Bennet*	37
2. Resist! *Meg Llewellyn*	55
3. Pride vs. Prejudice *Kenneth McIntosh*	71
4. The Call to Take a Stand *Ellyn Sanna*	91
5. The Inner Battle *Marjorie Bennet*	101

6. Building a Just Society *Lilly Weichberger & Kenneth McIntosh*	121
7. Facing the Opposition *Bruce Epperly*	137
8. The Power of Hope *Meg Llewellyn*	149
9. We're Stronger Together *Marjorie Bennet*	169
10. Persist! *Ellyn Sanna*	189
11. Ways to Get Involved	209
12. The Inspiration of Others' Lives	229
Reading Notes	297
Contributors	311

> I can not do everything,
> but I can do something.
> I must not fail to do the something
> that I can do.
>
> —Helen Keller

> I swore never to be silent whenever and wherever human beings endure suffering and humiliation. We must always take sides. Neutrality helps the oppressor, never the victim.
>
> —Elie Wiesel

HOW TO READ THIS BOOK

First, a note on our use of the word "Celtic" in the subtitle and throughout this book:

"Celtic" is the sort of word that means many things to different people. Its usage as a term for a particular type of spirituality often grates on historians, understandably, since the Celts were never a politically unified people; they never had a form of organized religion; and, like all human beings, they were (and are) a mixed bag of prejudice and tolerance, violence and compassion, misogyny and affirmation of women.

(The things the historical Celts truly seem to have had in common are a love of Nature and all creatures, a vital belief in the Otherworld, and an inspired creativity that wove through their artwork and stories.)

There are many books out there—some published by Anamchara Books—that can tell you more about the historical *Keltoi*, but for the purposes of this book, "Celtic" refers to a specific quality of spirituality that is founded on the tradition, mythology, and yes, some history, of a group of people who have lived since the Bronze Age in what we know now as the British Isles, the Isle of Man, and Brittany.

We use the word "Celtic" in our books because this form of spirituality speaks with a compelling relevancy to modern-day Pagans and Christians alike, particularly, perhaps, followers of Jesus who are disillusioned with the forms of organized Christianity at work in the world today. At the same time, we want to affirm that the spiritual characteristics so often labeled "Celtic" are not unique to Celtic culture and tradition. They are particularly shared by many forms of indigenous spirituality, including that found in Africa, Australia, and the Americas. "Celtic spirituality," however, is a term that's more familiar to the average reader.

Secondly, this book contains four main elements, which build on this understanding of Celtic spirituality:

- ❖ *Original essays by theologians and authors who have written other books on Celtic spirituality.* These personal essays connect various aspects of activism with the Celtic tradition, both Christian and Pagan.

- ❖ *A sprinkling of quotations from the world's great activists, people who have made a difference by resisting and persisting.* These quotes, which are taken from both speeches and books, are scattered throughout the text. The people who wrote and spoke these words were, in general, not "Celtic" in the sense that we've just defined—but their comments inspire us with practical ways to contribute to our communities. We encourage readers to ponder these small bites of wisdom. Skim over them if you like as you read the chapters' main text, but then go back through and allow each one to truly speak to you. Open yourself to seeing how they may be applied to your own life. The individuals to whom these words belong have given their lives to the cause of justice. They know from experience what works and what doesn't. They also know firsthand both the internal and external challenges of this work. In short, they're not just throwing out interesting ideas. They know what they're talking about.

- *A sampling of ideas and organizations* for getting started as an activist who resists . . . and persists.

- *Brief biographies of each individual whose words are included as quotations.* Not all of these individuals are what we traditionally consider to be activists, and yet through their vocations, whether as poets, priests, or politicians, they too spoke out for justice. As already mentioned, most are not specifically "Celtic activists," because the call to justice encompasses all nationalities, all religions, all societies—and the Celts would have been the first to view their work from a perspective that lacked any of these boundaries.

Reading these biographies not merely offers factual information but also inspiration. We can be encouraged as we better understand the realities these individuals experienced—the challenges they faced both within themselves and from the outside world in which they lived. We tend to think of people like Martin Luther King Jr., Mahatma Gandhi, Susan B. Anthony, and all the other great voices for justice as an elite group to which we could never belong. Their biographies help us to understand that we cannot be excused from taking a stand for justice because of our insignificance, timidity, or lack of skills. We are all called to persistently resist injustice wherever we encounter it. We cannot wait for the next Martin Luther King Jr. to step up, nor can we tell ourselves we must first gain more self-confidence, more knowledge, or more respect.

As feminist activist Audre Lorde wrote in *Sister Outsider,* "we have been socialized to respect fear . . . and while we wait in silence for that final luxury of fearlessness, the weight of that silence will choke us." Ultimately, helplessness is our most common excuse for not "becoming involved"—but in reality, we all have power. Each of us has a voice (of one sort or another) that can be used to build a better world. Let us walk in the footsteps of those who already have had the courage to act, learning from their lives and words.

❖ *And finally, at the back of the book, reading notes,* where you can find the sources of the quotes included in these pages.

> It is the true duty of all persons
> to promote the happiness
> of their fellow creatures
> to the utmost of their power.
> —William Wilberforce

> If you are neutral in situations of injustice, you have chosen the side of the oppressor. If an elephant has its foot on the tail of a mouse and you say that you are neutral, the mouse will not appreciate your neutrality.
>
> —Desmond Tutu

INTRODUCTION

❖❖❖

Ellyn Sanna

> If you think you are too small
> to make a difference,
> try sleeping with a mosquito.
>
> —the Dalai Lama

*Action is the stream,
and contemplation is the spring.*
—Thomas Merton

As a publisher that focuses on Celtic and mystic spirituality, why have we created a book on social activism? At first glance, the topic may seem to fall outside our normal realm—but we want to change that perspective. Mysticism and activism go hand in hand.

Our mission at Anamchara Books is "to create books with an inclusive spirituality that will build bridges between human beings, between humans and the environment, and most of all, between human beings and the Divine." In other words, we aim to publish books that encourage an inner spirituality that expresses itself in active involvement with others.

At Anamchara Books, we have defined Celtic spirituality as possessing these eight qualities:

- ❖ HOPE: The Divine asks that we look first for the good rather than the evil in all things.

- ❖ ENVIRONMENTAL STEWARDSHIP: The Earth is holy, and we have a Divine call to care for the living things with whom we share our planet.

- ❖ HOLISM: Dualistic concepts of good versus bad and spiritual versus physical are deceptive, for the sacred is present in all times and places; we cannot compartmentalize life.

- ❖ DIVINE IMMANENCE: God (regardless of what metaphors we may use for the Divine Spirit) is present in Nature, in humanity, and in all things.

❖ LOVE OF THE ARTS: Human creativity, expressed in words, shapes, movement, and music, has the power to form inspired connections between humans and the Divine.

- ❖ MYSTERY: The world is full of wonder—things that are beyond our comprehension—and the Otherworld is just next door.

- ❖ HOSPITALITY: We are called to welcome the stranger—into our land, our homes, and our hearts—no matter who she is or what he looks like.

- ❖ EQUALITY: All of us—regardless of our skin color, gender, age, politics, religion, or any other factor—are valuable; we are each necessary pieces contributing to a cosmic community.

These are all lovely qualities that have been discussed in multiple books on Celtic spirituality—but we don't always make the connection between these and the call to justice. Celtic spirituality is not simply a doorway into a mystical green world inhabited by wondrous beings, and it is not a pleasant fairy tale that makes us feel better about God and the world. Instead, the very nature of Celtic spirituality is a call for practical hard work in the real world. These beliefs challenge us to examine how we live them out in the ordinary realm of human interaction, with all its many societal and political problems. They call us to work for justice by actively saying no to things as they are, while we say yes to a world built on inclusion, equality, and fairness.

Following in the footsteps of the ancient Celts requires a spiritual outlook that includes accepting responsibility for our current world. It insists that we cannot be faithful to God if we are not faithful to our entire community (a community that not only includes humans, but also animals, plants, and the entire Earth). It is a mystical experience of the Divine that expresses itself in acts of tangible justice and compassion. As Pope Francis has said, "Prayer that does not lead you to practical action for . . . the poor, the sick, those in need of help . . . is a sterile and incomplete prayer."

The question then becomes: How do we take practical action on behalf of others? Acts of individual kindness and hospitality are certainly part of our calling as spiritual beings, no matter our specific beliefs. Using our financial resources is yet another obligation we should feel—putting our wallet where our mouths are (in a variety of ways), when it comes to our concerns for others. And last, as people who strive to walk in the footsteps of the Celtic saints (both Christian and Pagan), our spiritual life calls us to political involvement. What these three qualities look like in *your* life is something you alone can answer.

And yet many of us are uncomfortable connecting politics and spirituality. To speak of both in the same breath seems at best to be a tasteless faux pas. At worst, it threatens to infringe on one of America's hallowed constitutional protections, the separation of church and state.

These objections, however, are based on simplistic assumptions about what politics are. We have limited our understanding of this topic to the narrow slice of our lives that occurs when we step into an election booth. We equate politics with the struggle between political parties, and we reduce "political involvement" to identification with one of those parties. At its most primary level, though, the word "politics" is defined simply as the process of making decisions that apply to all members of a group. It involves the distribution of power and resources within a community, as well as the interrelationships within and without that community. This is the bottom line for all lawmaking and policy.

In a democracy, lawmaking and policy rest mostly in the hands of elected officials. As a result, we may tend to think that we have little power beyond our right to vote. However, political thinkers have known since at least the Roman Republic that an effective democracy requires an active citizenry.

Alexis de Tocqueville, the nineteenth-century political scientist, warned against "individualism," which he defined as that "calm and considered feeling which disposes each citizen to isolate himself from the mass of his fellows and withdraw into the circle of family and friends; with this little society formed to his taste, he gladly leaves the greater society to look after itself." Many of us have felt the temptation to do just that. If we are temperamentally uncomfortable with conflict, if we feel powerless, if we are pessimists and naysayers (and we all are each of these things to some extent, at one time or another), then we are drawn toward taking shelter with those who think like we do. Why try to change a resistant world when it's so much easier to withdraw into our comfortable enclaves? De Tocqueville cautioned, however, that if everyone were to take this route, there would be no one to keep tabs on the government—no one to ensure that the government represents the best interests of all citizens, both ourselves and those who are most vulnerable.

Perhaps we need to find a new way to think about politics, one that reaches past political parties and the labels of conservative and liberal. We need to step away from our personal identification with "our party" (which isn't much different from "our team") and instead focus on how we can actively work together for the common good of all members of our community. This is the sort of political activism in which the world's greatest leaders have engaged (people like Martin Luther King Jr. and Gandhi, Harriet Tubman and Rosa Parks).

Political activism asks us to speak out on behalf of each other, to insist on justice for all members of our society. If we seek to follow the universal Golden Rule—to do unto others as we would have them do to us—then activism is something with which we should all be vitally concerned. And for those of us intent on following a spiritual path connected with Celtic mythology and history, the call to activism cannot be avoided. In the words of activist, author, and scholar Anna Julia Cooper:

> Religion (ought to be if it isn't) a great deal more than mere gratification of the instinct for worship linked with the straight-teaching of irreproachable credos. Religion must be life made true; and life is action, growth, development—begun now and ending never. And a life made true cannot confine itself—it must reach out and twine around every pulsing interest within reach of its uplifting tendrils.

Celtic spirituality has this quality of green and living dynamism. It calls us to be faithful to something far deeper and more inclusive than mere doctrine. It challenges us to experience a "life made true"—active, growing, eternal life that reaches out to all Creation.

The ancient Celts' connection with the supernatural Otherworld was what inspired them to be active participants in the ordinary, everyday world. They would have understood what poet Countee Cullen wrote in the twentieth century: "The truth is . . . everything counts. Everything. Everything we do and everything we say. Everything helps or hurts." There is no true boundary line between the "spiritual" and the "physical."

While the twenty-first century offers us challenges the Celtic saints never encountered, there is much we can learn from their world view. Regardless of the factual historicity of the stories that have been passed down to us, the embedded meaning within these tales continues to inspire and enlighten, today as much it always has in past centuries.

In the nineteenth century, Alexander Carmichael collected ancient oral traditions from the rural Scots, who seemed to still consider the Celtic saints as living, friendly companions in their ordinary lives. A woman named Isabel Mac Eachainn told Carmichael a story about Saint Columba (also known as Calum Cille) that illustrates the quality of practical, compassionate action that the saints extended to everyone they encountered.

> A widow woman at Tabal, Mull, had a cow ill with the *tarbhan* [swelling from surfeit], and she was wringing her hands and beating her breast to see her beloved cow in pain. At that moment she saw Calum Cille and his twelve disciples in their *curachan* [little boat or coracle], rowing home to Iona. The widow ran down to the *rudha* [point] and hailed Calum Cille, and asked him to heal her cow. Calum Cille never turned a dull ear to the poor, to the penitent, to the distressed, and he came ashore and made the *ora* [prayer] for the white cow, and the white cow rose upon her feet and shook herself and began to browse upon the green grass before her.

Columba told the woman to go home with confidence in both God and her own self. "And all will go well with thee and with thy cow." Having said this, Columba rejoined his followers in the curachan and resumed his journey.

"There was no one like Calum Cille, no one, my dear," Isabel Mac Eachainn told Carmichael. "He was big and handsome and eloquent, haughty to the over-haughty and humble to the humble, kind to the weak and wounded." Healing a cow with swollen udders may not seem like the sort of activism with which we are familiar today, but this story illustrates the Celtic saints' active compassion for even the most seemingly mundane needs. Their connection with the invisible Otherworld was what inspired them to be unflagging participants in the everyday, visible world.

Their spirituality was not a passive one where they folded their hands in prayer and isolated themselves from the rest of the world; instead, saints like Columba withdrew in times of solitude and prayer so that they might then go out and engage in more effective and compassionate action.

The Celts were truly activists for justice. They not only healed cows; they also persuaded kings to change their policies; they stood up for women and others who were endangered by prejudice; and they worked with tireless love on behalf of all of Earth's creatures. They resisted the injustice of their day—and they persisted throughout their entire lifetimes, until their deaths. (And some would say that they are still hard at work fighting injustice from the Otherworld.)

For the Celtic Christians, activism was not a sometime thing, an activity to be engaged in now and then when it was convenient. Instead, it was the constant, lived expression of their connection to God, humans, and the Earth. It was life itself.

In Krista Tippett's book *Becoming Wise,* she wrote, "Change has always happened in the margins. . . . Seismic shifts in common life, as in geophysical reality, begin in spaces and cracks." The Celts were people who lived on the margins, at the very rim of what they considered to be the known world, and they too believed that marginal places can crack open in powerful and startling ways.

Today, the Celts' voices call to us down through the centuries, challenging us to follow in their footsteps into the edges of our world, the places where people don't fit easily, where we tend to draw boundary lines between "us" and "them," where we lack the comforting certainty of the majority. There is work to be done there, on the margins.

Let us begin!

> Practice goodness. Demand justice. Give guidance to those who lean toward violence. Be an advocate for vulnerable children and women.
> —Isaiah 1:17

I
WHAT IS JUSTICE?

Marjorie Bennet

> We must mend
> what has been torn apart,
> make justice imaginable again,
> in a world so obviously unjust
>
> —Albert Camus.

> *Justice that love gives is a surrender,*
> *justice that law gives is a punishment.*
> —Mahatma Gandhi

Some twenty-four centuries ago, when the Celts were still wandering across southern Europe, a Celtic woman named Onomaris brought justice to her people. The band of nomads to which she belonged had been starving, on the brink of death, when the women of the tribe decided that something had to be done. They gathered together and demanded that someone lead them to a land where they could safely provide for their families. The women promised to swear allegiance to whomever would take on this responsibility.

But when the warriors heard the women's request, they exchanged uneasy glances; they muttered among themselves and shifted their weight from foot to foot while they nervously fingered their weapons. Eventually, it became clear that no man was willing to accept the women's challenge. Instead, Onomaris, her red hair blowing behind her like a flag, stepped forward.

"I will lead you," she said.

The first thing Onomaris did was to reorganize her people. "From now on," she told them, "no one among us will be wealthy. No one will have more privileges than anyone else. Everything we have will be shared, so that no one goes hungry and no one lacks clothing against the cold."

The people knew Onomaris's courage and intelligence. They trusted her. And so everyone brought forward whatever goods they possessed and placed them on the ground before her.

When everything was there, Onomaris sorted through the piles of belongings, and then she redistributed them. She gave each family only the supplies of food, animals, and weapons they needed for the journey that lay ahead.

Then, having freed her people from quarreling, greed, and inequity, she led her tribe north across the Danube River in search of a new home. Eventually, Onomaris brought her people to a peaceful and prosperous land where she ruled with justice and wisdom.

This story, based on the ancient Greek work *Tractatus de Mulieribus*, is one of the earliest depictions of a Celtic woman found in historical records. I love Onomaris because she embodies the woman I want to be—creative, courageous, strong, and compassionate. If I were to encounter a similar situation, however, I'm not sure I would demonstrate the wisdom and justice she did. As someone who grew up in the "#metoo" era, I suspect I would have been intimidated by the possibility of blowback from all those male warriors. My worries about offending my friends and family would have hampered my ability to lead my community on such a radically new path. I'm grateful, though, to Onomaris for challenging me to live up to her example. I think of her as a spiritual companion—a sort of personal saint, if you like—pointing me over and over toward strength and courage in the fight for justice.

Her name is thought to come from the ancient word for "rowan tree." She may have earned that name simply because of her red hair (*rowan* means "red" in the old languages—which might equally have been a reference to Onomaris's menstrual blood as a symbol of her valiant womanhood), but her name may also have indicated her symbolic connection to what the Celts considered to be the Tree of Life—the rowan, which represented courage, wisdom, and justice. This tree was often the sacred heart of a community, the place where kings were crowned, laws enacted, and

important announcements made. It symbolized the living connections between community members. As the Tree of Life, the rowan also signified the way in which the invisible spiritual world and the visible world of daily life were interconnected, a single verdant organism.

Onomaris's story is also one of our first historical glimpses of the Celtic concept of justice. The Old Celtic word usually translated as "justice" was *kouéro*, which meant "in accordance with the truth." The Celts' idea of Truth (with a capital T) was far more than either personal integrity or an absence of falsehood. Instead, it referred to a cosmic, indisputable rightness that human behavior must seek to imitate. It meant living out in practice, as Onomaris did, the green and breathing relationship between Heaven and Earth and between community members.

Connected to the Celtic concept of justice was the idea of honor, which referred to the individual's expression of Truth. In all the old Celtic languages

(Gaelic, Welsh, Cornish, and Breton), the word used for "honor" came from the same word as "face."

Today, we are familiar with the phrase "saving face," but as Westerners, most of us fail to grasp what this phrase truly means. We connect it with an ego-centered reluctance to be personally embarrassed. When we "save face," we think, we manage to maintain our sense of dignity and importance. The ancient Celts, however, understood this idea somewhat differently. In a culture where everything was related to communal relationships, "face" was the term for personal, individual identity—what we usually call the "self"—existing within the larger community. This is the meaning contained within Jesus' words in the Gospel of Thomas when he says, "What was your original face before your mother and father were born?" Jesus is talking here about an idea that was difficult to grasp in the ancient world—a sense of unique identity that did not depend on any community or kinship relationship.

For the Celts, to have a face—an individual identity—required personal integrity, which was a quality that depended on how you lived out your relationships with others. People or things that were your responsibility or under your protection were referred to as being "on" or "under" your face, essential to your own identity. To have a face, then, meant being a person of Truth, a person who embodied cosmic *rightness,* who practiced justice in all her interactions. Without these healthy and just relationships, individual honor and even individual identity were impossible.

All this may seem as though I'm getting caught up in a purely academic discussion of etymology. I believe, however, that the Celts give us a corrective view on justice, one that's desperately needed in our world today, where we tend to think of justice as something that happens *outside* our interior sense of our selves, something legal and societal, pertaining to the authority of the government, rather than something that is intimate, personal, and relational.

Our current definition of justice has more to do with the administration of consequences for law-breaking. It tends to be punitive. Lady Justice, who symbolizes our concept of the judicial system, not only wears a blindfold (representing her impartiality), but she also holds scales, with which she measures guilt and innocence, and a sword, representing her swift and final authority to mete out punishment for wrongdoing. Crime is an act against the state, a violation of a law, rather than an act that hurts another person or the community as a whole.

The Celtic concept of justice, however, was much different. The Irish Brehon Laws give us a detailed record of the practical realities of this system. Scholars have a hard time agreeing on either the origins or translation of these laws, but we do know that they are far more ancient than the first eighth-century written record we have of them. Some Celtic scholars go so far as to say that the Brehon Laws are rooted in the same primeval source as the Hindu Laws of Manu (which date back a millennium before the Common Era). Regardless of their age, what the Brehon Laws clearly reveal is that anything that disrupted the community—even the most trivial offense—was dangerous to the entire community's well-being. The laws laid out specific ways in which damage could be restored, rifts healed, and relationships reconciled.

This concept of justice is what modern-day thinkers refer to as "restorative justice" (as opposed to "retributive justice"). According to retributive-justice thinking, it is the criminal justice system's job to control crime, whereas restorative justice gives that job to the community as a whole. Accountability for wrongdoing does not mean submitting to punishment, as it does in retributive justice, but rather taking action to repair harm. The wrongdoer is not defined by guilt but by the ability to be reintegrated back into the community through work and problem solving. Restorative justice puts the emphasis on building a better future rather than on punishment for deeds done in the past.

The Celtic saints integrated this approach into their communities, building their "Penitentials" on many of the same principles as had been found in the Brehon Laws. Much like the Brehon Laws, the Penitentials were detailed lists of ordinary daily-life transgressions paired with steps to bring about reparation and reconciliation. The Celtic followers of Christ perceived "sin" as a disease to be healed, rather than a crime to be punished—and it was a disease that hurt not only the individual but the entire network of relationships that formed the community as a whole.

These ideas about justice endured for centuries in the Celtic world, despite the imposition of the English legal system. Justice continued to be thought of as a way to restore harmony within the community, as indicated by this Scottish prayer Alexander Carmichael recorded at the beginning of the twentieth century:

> Peace between neighbors, peace between kindred, peace between lovers, in love of the King of life.

Peace between person and person, peace between husband and wife, peace between parents and children, the peace of Christ above all peace.

The prayer concludes with these lines, which harken back to the ancient concept of "face": "Bless, O Christ, my face, and let my face bless everything." Individual identity—personal Truth—is still intertwined with "rightness" in relationship with both the Divine and the entire world.

Historians suspect that the reason restorative justice endured longer in Scotland than in other places in the Western world was that it was a region where central, federal government was weak and local kin networks remained strong. Ian Whyte in *Scotland Before the Industrial Revolution* tells us that in nineteenth century Scotland, settlements for serious crimes often involved formal public reconciliations as part of a religious service, once again connecting the individual, the community, and the Divine.

The Celtic concept of restorative justice was not unique to them, of course; other indigenous groups, including the Maori and Native Americans, had similar practices. Communities that live close to the land and each other seem to have a better understanding of justice than we do in our "advanced" technological society. The Celtic Christians connected this sense of communal justice to their call to follow Christ.

I grew up in a church that told me that the justice of God referred to "His" need to punish sin, and that Jesus came to "save" us from this punishment. Today, however, my reading of the Gospels shows me instead the Jesus the Celts saw: concerned with building the Realm of God in concrete ways that included delivering the poor and vulnerable from political and social oppression, welcoming the outcast and marginalized, redistributing resources fairly so that there was enough for all, healing the sick and wounded, and building a practical peace that put an end to violence of all kinds, whether physical or verbal. That, I believe, was Jesus' concept of justice, and it is one reason, when the Pagan Celts first encountered the Christ-story, that it resonated so strongly with them. This was a perspective on life they already understood.

In the sixth century, the Irish monk Columbanus recommended that we be careful not to "paint a false image" over our own faces, turning our true selves into hollow phantoms rather than the luminescent, living image of God. When it came to claiming our true identities as God-images, Columbanus saw no room for shades of gray. "For truth is distinct from falsehood," he said in one of his sermons, and "justice from unrighteousness, love from ill-will, enthusiasm from apathy, straightness from crookedness, affection from fake-love." Each of these qualities, said Columbanus, "paints an image upon us," and "justice and injustice, peace and disagreement, are mutually opposed to one another."

Columbanus concluded his sermon by saying, "Let Christ paint his image on us, as he means when he says, 'My peace I give you, My peace I leave to you.' . . . We must be occupied by nothing but love." In other words, justice and love are ultimately the same thing.

Two centuries earlier than Columbanus, the Celtic theologian known as Pelagius (and also as Morgan of Wales) wrote:

> Those people are Christians who are merciful to all, who are not motivated by injustice, who cannot endure the oppression of the poor before their very eyes, who come to the aid of the wretched, who help the needy, who sorrow with those who mourn, who feel the suffering of others as if it were their own . . . and at whose hands no one suffers injustice.

What Pelagius made clear is that justice is not impersonal or abstract. It is as personal and intimate as love. And as a follower of Jesus, that is the justice I am called to pursue. I may lack the confidence and strength that Onomaris demonstrated—but that does not excuse me.

I cannot profess to work for justice if I am occupied by anything but love—the practical, muscular love that is up-close, responsive, and immediate. This sort of love is not easy, nor does it come naturally to my ego-driven tendencies. Nevertheless, that is the real meaning of justice, and I cannot be my true self—wearing my true face—unless I seek justice in all my interactions

> Think about it: virtually every atrocity in the history of humankind was enabled by a populace that turned away from a reality that seemed too painful to face, while virtually every revolution for peace and justice has been made possibly by a group of people who chose to bear witness and demanded that others bear witness as well.
>
> —Melanie Joy

II
RESIST!

Meg Llewellyn

> During times of universal deceit
> telling the truth becomes
> a revolutionary act.
>
> —George Orwell

> *I cannot stand to be conformist,*
> *I don't accept what is, I like to say no.*
>
> —Elie Wiesel

"Resist!" is a common battle cry these days, calling us to work against all that is negative in our government and society. When I hear the word "resistance," however, the first image that enters my mind is not protestors marching in Washington, DC, or picketers with signs outside a corrupt corporation's doors. I don't think of an underground military faction fighting for independence either. No, when I imagine what resistance looks like, I think first of Jesus—multiplying loaves and fishes, turning water into wine, healing the sick and disabled, and walking on water. In each of these miracle stories, Jesus resisted this world's status quo. He refused to be bound by its rules.

To resist, Merriam Webster tells me, means to withstand the force or effect of something. The word comes from Latin roots: against (*re-*) + to stand firm (*sistere*). I was interested to discover that "persist" has a similar etymology; its Latin roots are: thoroughly, with forward movement (*per-*) + to stand firm (*sistere*). In other words, you could say that both resisting and persisting require taking a stand—but persistence is resistance carried out in such a thorough way that it reaches forward into the future. This is the resistance of Christ.

Jesus changed the world forever each time he withstood the force of the world's logic and expectations. By doing the seemingly impossible, he proved that society, tradition, politics, and government need not have the final say. He said, "No!" to injustice and poverty and hatred. His miracles were acts of resistance.

Personally, I believe the Gospels' accounts actually happened, but you don't have to consider the miracles of Christ to be literal truth to grasp the deeper truth that underlies them. The point of all these stories isn't that Jesus was a wonderworker, a sort of holy magician who performed amazing feats of miraculous power. Instead, the real meaning behind these stories is what they tell us about the Realm of Heaven—that it's a place of limitless compassion and active generosity, a place of justice and equality, where even the most seemingly insignificant people are treasured and cared for.

Jesus taught that the Realm of Heaven is not the after-life but rather the now-life. According to Jesus, the only rule that governs this now-and-present Heaven is love (Matthew 22:37,39). By refusing to obey this world's rules—as demonstrated in his miracles—he embodied a form of radical resistance that can serve as a template for us all. He took his stand on Heaven's ground.

The Celtic saints made Christ's template for resistance their own. Like him, they refused to obey the dictates of power and wealth, tradition and society. They lived their lives according to Heaven's rule, resisting their world's societal and cultural norms. When confronted with worldly demands and expectations, they simply disregarded them.

Brigid is a prime example of the Celtic saints' joyous resistance. She is famous for her stubborn disregard of all the expectations placed on her by the wealthy establishment of her day. Brigid fearlessly obeyed the law of love, trusting God to deal with the consequences of her actions.

In Celtic lands, people who still tell stories about Brigid sound as though they are as familiar with the goddess-saint as many of us are with Oprah or some other well-loved celebrity. One of these old stories tells of the time Brigid went to help her mother, who was in service to a wealthy man. Since her mother was sick, Brigid took over her work in the dairy. The rest of the story goes something like this:

When Brigid churned the butter, she always divided it into thirteen parts. The first twelve portions were in honor of the twelve apostles, but the thirteenth part—which she would make as big again as all the rest—was to the honor of Christ. That part she would give to strangers and to the poor.

But the man who owned the farm got word that Brigid was giving away his milk and butter, and so he and his wife came to visit the farm. They found the cows to be contented and the calves fat, but the wife was suspicious. She had brought in their wagon an enormous vessel that was as tall as her husband, and now she said to Brigid, "See that this vessel is filled to the brim with butter."

Brigid knew that she only had a little butter left, since she had given away all the rest earlier that morning to a family of strangers who had come to the dairy's door, but she said nothing, only nodded and went into the kitchen. When she was alone, she prayed, "O my High Prince, who can do all these things, bless my kitchen with your right hand! My kitchen, the kitchen of the bright Lord, the white God; a kitchen that is blessed by my King; a kitchen where there is butter. My Friend is coming, the Son of Mary, and he will bless my kitchen, that there may be plenty with Him." After she had prayed, she brought out the small pot of butter that was all she had left and rejoined the owner and his wife.

When the wife saw the small amount of butter Brigid had in her pot, she said, "Do you resist my command, girl? Why do you offer me such a small portion of butter?"

Brigid smiled at the woman. "I do resist you and your husband, for you have no concern for those whose need is greater than yours. But the Son of Mary will see to it that there is plenty for you as well." With that, she dumped the butter and whey into the enormous vessel.

The owner's wife laughed. "You cannot hope to fool us, girl! I'd like to see how you think to fill such a large vessel with such a small bit of butter and whey! You should be punished for your disobedience, giving away what wasn't yours to give."

But Brigid still smiled. "I gave away only what belonged to Christ. And now God will add something to what I give back to you."

Brigid's butter and whey poured out into the enormous vessel in a steady stream that never ended until the vessel was brimming over. The owner and his wife grumbled to themselves, for they knew that Brigid had gotten the best of them—but what could they do?

I'm sure Brigid had a reputation as a troublemaker. She refused to let hunters kill the animals they were pursuing, she gave away her father's bacon to a dog and his sword to a poor man, she plucked out her eye rather than marry the man her father had chosen for her, and she tricked the King of Leinster into giving her a large portion of land for her monastery. She was certainly not the meek and submissive woman that some forms of modern Christianity insist is what God wants!

In the old stories, Brigid, like Jesus, tapped into a supernatural stream of power, but the miracles she worked are not as important as what they tell us about who she was and what she stood for. She stood for the poor, the vulnerable, the broken, the outcast. She stood for love and compassion and generosity. She stood for God and the Divine Realm. With each act of resistance, she planted her feet firmly on Heaven's ground.

Stubborn and inquisitive, loving and joyful, annoying and generous, courageous and outspoken—that

was Brigid! She was a woman of both compassion and integrity, who refused to be taken in by lies or accept hatred as the status quo. While others fell in line behind power and wealth, Brigid held her ground. She spoke the truth even if no one wanted to hear it, and she faced down danger with the confident power of love.

When I listen to the old stories about her, she reminds me of the advice L. M. Browning gives in her book *Seasons of Contemplation: A Book of Midnight Meditations*:

> Question everything—no matter how beloved, or how long-held, or how exalted—without apology. Only those who build their world upon lies need fear an inquisitive mind. The truth will remain, even after a storm of doubt and revolution has washed over it. Only illusions need be protected. The truth . . . existed before us and will continue to exist after us.

Brigid and the other Celtic saints knew that Divine love is a reality far truer than any "facts" or assumptions worldly power can ever offer. They believed the Divine Realm was a real and living world in which we are constantly immersed, whether we know it or not. They chose to build their lives there.

We too can make that choice, but this requires first a total shift in the way we look at life. It doesn't mean that we turn away from the visible world with all its neediness and ugliness but that instead we view it differently. We shake free of our indifference and instead care passionately about the world around us.

Author, activist, and Holocaust survivor Elie Wiesel wrote,

> In the face of suffering, one has no right to turn away, not to see. In the face of injustice, one may not look the other way. When someone suffers, and it is not you, that person comes first. . . . To

watch over one who grieves is a more urgent duty than to think of God.

Elie Wiesel also wrote, "In order to fly, you have to give up the ground you are standing on." We might also say that in order to truly resist, we have to give up the ground we've been standing on, the ground we take for granted is reality—the foundation built by society and tradition, politics and government—and with Brigid and Jesus, choose instead to take our place on Heaven's ground.

With our feet dug into that holy soil, we can make our stand. As we resist the forces of indifference and greed and power, we can persist in building the visible Realm of Heaven

> This is what Yahweh says:
> "Accomplish justice and truth.
> Snatch from danger all those who
> have been robbed by the oppressor's
> power. And do not mistreat or do
> violence to strangers, nor to
> vulnerable children and women."
>
> —Jeremiah 22:3

> We can at least try to understand our own motives, passions, and prejudices, so as to be conscious of what we are doing.... This is very difficult, because our own prejudice and emotional bias always seems to us so rational.
>
> —T. S. Eliot

III

PRIDE VS PREJUDICE

Kenneth McIntosh

> Prejudice is a burden that confuses
> the past, threatens the future
> and renders the present inaccessible.
>
> —Maya Angelou

All our silences in the face of racist assault are acts of complicity.

—bell hooks

Celtic spirituality is like an ancient holy spring that pours forth restoring waters for modern believers and contemporary society. That is the premise of my book *Water from an Ancient Well,* which conveys the idea that Celtic spiritual practices—both Pagan and Christian—can be truly life-refreshing. Celtic concepts from the Early Middle Ages have helped many Christians to love God and serve neighbors with renewed joy. In a similar way, revivals of Celtic Paganism have enabled countless people to reconnect with the sacredness of their lives and the natural world. I walk this way daily and share it with others.

But even the very best things can be corrupted. Those of us who follow this sacred path must be vigilant, for there is the real possibility that the holy well of our faith can be infused with the spiritual and social poison of an intolerant—even hateful—superiority. Prejudice can disguise itself as pride.

This is especially a concern given the increasing harassment of minorities in America and in the UK. As I write this, the local news has reported threats and loud verbal attacks against people in three churches that welcome LGBTQ+ people. At the same time, in the same locale, a Middle Eastern bakery was repeatedly vandalized, and Muslim students were harassed on a local campus and in the adjacent community.

These are merely the incidents that came to my attention within the narrow circles of my relationships; they are microcosms of larger national and international trends. Tragically, the increasing prominence of blatant racism and the normalizing of hate crimes threatens to push back the gains in equality achieved in the past decades. There is growing atmosphere where people are emboldened to put prejudice in action with threats and violence.

In an article titled "White Nationalism and the Ethics of Medieval Studies," Sierra Lomuto addresses fellow scholars of medieval studies, but her concerns are equally relevant for those of us who embrace Celtic spirituality (both Pagan and Christian). In her article, Lomuto says, "There should be no doubt that they [white nationalists] will reach us in our bubble of academia. They will likely reach us medievalists first."

Personally, I'm concerned that the Celtic genres of religious life could also be on the front line of racist activism. As Lomuto points out, there is "deep significance of Celtic iconography within the white nationalist community." She goes on to say that "Stormfront [is] a white nationalist online community whose tag line reads, 'We are the voice of the new, embattled White minority' and whose emblem is the "sun-cross" version of the Celtic Cross.' In fact, one of the site's message boards . . . asks for tattoo ideas and [gives] the advice that Celtic crosses work better for tattoos because they are not as obvious as a swastika."

Symbols are multivalent; that is both their beauty and their vulnerability. The swastika is a case in point; in Vedic religion, it was a symbol of good fortune, in Buddhism, a symbol of the Dharma wheel, and in indigenous Southwestern American cultures it was the "rolling log" of the solar calendar—all life-affirming meanings for a symbol that has come to be perceived as the symbol of genocide and utter evil.

It sickens me that the Celtic wheel cross can be coopted for similar insidious ends. In its pre-Christian forms (for example, the standing stones at Callanish and other ancient sites) the wheel cross represented the turning solar cycle of the fourfold Celtic year, with its natural rhythms of daily life and quarterly celebrations. For medieval Celtic Christians, the wheel cross symbolized God's love that spreads like sunshine, "embracing the earth, the sea, the winds and the sky, and everything else believed to exist far away" (in the words of ninth-century Irish theologian John Scottus Eriugena). In both its Pagan and Christian meanings, the wheel cross is a symbol of universal inclusivity. When used as a signifier of any sort of human superiority, its meaning is utterly and tragically upended.

As people of goodwill, we must now share a heightened urgency to combat hatred and intolerance. We dare not think, "Others might use the same symbols that I use to express their prejudice, but that's not what it means for me, so I can ignore that." Each of us has the sacred duty to speak out against the hijacking of our cherished images, and the absolute obligation to forcefully confront and denounce prejudice if it comes anywhere near our camp. Those who share the sacred well must ensure that its life-giving waters remain free from poison.

In this time of cultural crisis, there is a moral mandate for each of us who love the Celtic ways to do the following:

- ❖ Recognize that appreciation for one's heritage contains the potential for poisonous claims of superiority.

- ❖ Proclaim the inclusive nature of Celtic spirituality.

- ❖ Admit that historically Celts have not been immune from perpetrating racism and prejudice.

- ❖ Educate regarding the influence and presence of people of diverse racial and cultural origins in the Celtic lands in the Early Middle Ages (both historically and mythologically).

We need to be wary of the fine line between pride in one's heritage and prejudiced claims of superiority.

All people can take pride in their respective cultural backgrounds; to do so is recognition of the fact that the Divine image manifests in rainbow splendor throughout the Earth. People are wonderfully made, not in general but in local and specific ways. But healthy appreciation of one's lineage becomes cancerous when the first hint of superiority creeps in (and we are each susceptible to the ego's inflated claims).

Sierra Lomuto rightly points out in her article, "To celebrate one's Irish, German, or Italian ethnicity is akin to celebrating one's Ethiopian, Chilean, or Thai ethnicity. There is no equation to be made between whiteness and ethnic heritage. Whiteness is a racial category of privileged dominance; it is a power structure upheld by the oppression and marginalization of non-whiteness."

Prejudice can be perceived in the resistance some viewers expressed when the BBC series *Merlin* cast Angel Coulby, an accomplished English actress with darker skin than that of her fellow cast members, in the role of Guinevere; yet this casting decision provides an important lesson in the distinction between racial and cultural identity. Guinevere's character acted according to the same norms and beliefs as the other characters on the show. Her presence was a disavowal of the false connection between pigmentation and stereotyped cultural, social, or religious norms.

The attributes most valued by adherents of Celtic spirituality—such as harmony with Nature, connection between the physical and spiritual worlds, and mystical experiences—are in fact common to indigenous groups worldwide. "Celtic" Christianity has found enthusiastic reception in communities with predominantly black believers in Africa and among Christians in First Nation communities in North America, where the values listed on the previous pages are perceived as antidotes to colonialist versions of the Christian message. These "indigenous" values are by no means exclusive to pink-skinned people nor are they to people of browner pigmentation! They are the universal domain of people who originally lived in tune with the natural world (which is the root experience of *all* humans).

Both Pagan and Christian Celtic spiritualities focused on the concepts of welcome and broad inclusivity. It is obviously destructive—and a betrayal of the better natures of the Celtic past—to pair "Celtic" heritage, language, or practice with claims of superiority in terms of gender, religion, sexual orientation, or any of the other characteristics in which humans differ.

In pre-Christian Celtic communities, hospitality was a preeminent virtue. Although clans fought against clans throughout the Insular regions (what we know today as the British Islands), people recognized that cold and hunger were even deadlier foes—and so when visitors arrived in a Gaelic Iron Age village, they were fed and sheltered before any inquiry was made regarding their origins or affiliations.

Likewise, from the first origins of Celtic Christianity it was understood that Christ walked among humans in the form of the "stranger" as much as the familiar "friend." Like all great religions worldwide, the Christian faith of the Celts focused on the Golden Rule, treating one's neighbor as oneself. In both Pagan and Christian understanding, the great knotwork pattern that held all things together also tied together the vast diversity of human color and sound and shape within the immense mosaic of Divine creation.

The Celtic Christian neomonastic community of which I am a member, the Community of Aidan and Hilda, includes in its founding principles the mandate for "Healing Fragmented Peoples and Communities." Members of the community are encouraged to undertake initiatives for justice across divides of race, religion, language, and culture. In its introductory pamphlet, the Community states, "The Celtic way of mission is to be indigenous. The way of life can be translated into the idioms of your language, and should be applied in ways that express your distinctive culture." Other Celtic spiritual communities—both Pagan and Christian—have similar emphases that celebrate diversity and work for increasing inclusivity.

Although inclusivity is a vital part of Celtic spiritual tradition, people of Celtic heritage like me need to admit that racism and other forms of prejudice have also been part of our history. If we deny the evils of our past, then we are more likely to be complicit today. Furthermore, past injustices often require present-day deep apologies followed by reparations.

For example, I have a great personal affection for Robert Burns; I consider him akin to Shakespeare in greatness; he is part of my wife's family tree; and I appreciate his claims for human equality in "A Man's a Man for A' That" and other poems—and yet it's a historical fact that in 1786, when struggling financially, Burns almost wound up in charge of a slave plantation in Jamaica. Had he done so, he would have been one of many Scots who were slave owners in the Americas. Although Scots, Irish, and Welsh immigrants suffered many hardships and indignities in their journeys (especially the Irish), they were also at times perpetrators of injustice against other minorities, including African Americans, Native Americans, and indigenous Australians and New Zealanders. Prejudice is, unfortunately, a human disease to which no cultural or ethnic group is totally immune.

As people who follow a Celtic spiritual path, we also need to educate ourselves and others about the racial and cultural diversity that existed within the ancient Celtic world. For example, the Middle Eastern influence on Celtic spirituality in the Early Middle Ages is well-documented. Archaeologists have also established a sea trade route from the Middle East to fifth-century Tintagel in Cornwall, which is the alleged time and place of King Arthur's birth. Furthermore, entire communities of

Syrian Christians lived in Southern France in the fifth and sixth centuries, and the great Irish missionary Columbanus wrote of a Syrian woman whom he met in Europe. The Egyptian desert fathers Anthony and Paul of Thebes are depicted on the Scottish Ruthwell Cross, and there are Egyptian monks buried in a cemetery of the ancient Irish monastery on the Island of Innishmore. A recent archeological find is an ancient Irish codex that includes pieces of Egyptian papyrus.

Nor were the people of ancient Celtic lands uniformly pink skinned. The eleventh-century document titled "The Fragmentary Annals of Ireland" tells of a group of black Africans who settled in Ireland in the ninth century, having been transported there by Vikings; archaeological digs at three Gloucestershire grave sites, also from the ninth century, include three persons of African origins. Blacks also settled on the other side of the Irish Sea; according to a 2010 article in the *Guardian*:

One of the richest inhabitants of fourth-century Roman York . . . was a woman of black African ancestry. . . . "We're looking at a population mix which is much closer to contemporary Britain than previous historians had suspected," Hella Eckhardt, senior lecturer at the department of archaeology at Reading University, said. "In the case of York, the Roman population may have had more diverse origins than the city has now."

The same article in the *Guardian* reports proof of an even more ancient brown-skinned population in the British Isles. "Isotope evidence suggests that up to 20 percent of the residents of Celtic lands were descended from long-distance migrants. Some were African or had African ancestors."

Furthermore, geneticists have identified DNA previously found only in people from West Africa in more than a third of the white males in a northern

England community. Another genetic lineage is very common in North Wales that is usually found in places like North Africa and Ethiopia.

The Arthurian mythology of the High Middle Ages also includes people of color. The fourteenth-century *Romance of Morien* recounts the exploits of a character whose name indicates his Muslim religious background and whose skin color is repeatedly described as black. Perhaps the greatest rendering of Arthurian myth, Wolfram von Eschenbach's thirteenth-century German poem *Parzival,* includes Feirefis, who has a black father and white mother. In Eschenbach's story of the Holy Grail, Feirefis attains the Grail and marries the Grail bearer. Sir Palomides, in Sir Thomas Malory's definitive Arthurian account *Le Morte de Arthur,* is a dark-skinned Muslim.

When people of color show up in popular television and cinema renderings of medieval legends— such as Gwen in *Merlin,* as well as Nasir in *Robin of Sherwood* and Azeem in *Robin Hood Prince of Thieves*—some viewers have decried these depictions as attempts to "rewrite history" in order to "be more PC." On the contrary; as noted above, both racial and cultural diversity are reflected in the archaeology, written history, and mythology of medieval Europe. To exclude such persons from contemporary depictions is—in a double sense—whitewashing history.

As interest in Celtic spirituality continues to grow, we must work to prevent equating Celtic traditions and history with "whiteness," even implicitly. We must also safeguard against any destructive, egoic urge to claim the superiority of Celtic ways over other cultural and social traditions.

I am proud of all that is good about Celtic spirituality—but I do not forget that ultimately, any form of exclusion, any claim of superiority, and any willingness to allow injustice against others contradicts the core values of Celtic spirituality (as well as the core values of all the world's great spiritual traditions). Those of us who imbibe life-giving waters from the deep well of Celtic tradition must ensure that hatred and prejudice not contaminate our sacred springs.

> Our mission, therefore, is to confront ignorance with knowledge, bigotry with tolerance, and isolation with the outstretched hand of generosity. Racism can, will, and must be defeated.
>
> —Kofi Annan

> Cautious, careful people, always casting about to preserve their reputation and social standing, never can bring about a reform. Those who are really in earnest must be willing to be anything or nothing in the world's estimation ... and bear the consequences.
>
> —Susan B. Anthony

IV

THE CALL TO TAKE A STAND

Ellyn Sanna

Every time we turn our heads the other way when we see the law flouted, when we tolerate what we know to be wrong, when we close our eyes and ears to the corrupt because we are too busy or too frightened, when we fail to speak up and speak out, we strike a blow against freedom and decency and justice.

—Robert Kennedy

*It's not just about hope and ideas.
It's about action.*

—Shirin Ebadi

"You say you want a revolution," the Beatles sang in 1968. The song goes on to affirm that while we may want to change the world, destruction and violence are not the ways to achieve positive change.

It's hard to hold on to this understanding. Injustice makes us angry. Some of us use that anger to fuel positive action, but others of us cross the line from anger into hatred—while still others retreat from our anger, repressing it, frightened that it may lead us into conflict and violence. We'd rather stick our heads in the sand, refuse to read the news, and think happy thoughts within the comfort and safety of our homes. Not all of us are so privileged to have that option. Some of us are forced to live with injustice every day, an inescapable fact of life woven into our reality.

And yet hate is never an effective tool to inspire rebellion, because hate fuels war rather than social change. Still, apathy, fear, and ignorance are not much better. Having an ostrich mentality implicitly condones injustice. It is a selfish outlook that refuses to be disturbed by the plight of those who don't have the luxury of burying their heads to escape a harsh reality.

As someone who takes Celtic spirituality seriously, I believe I am called to actively participate in a global community, the "Body of Christ," a physical and spiritual interconnection between humans and between each element of our living world. This living relationship asks me to leave the mental comfort I've constructed for myself—and take a stand on behalf of justice. It asks me to be a rebel.

Recently, reading Albert Camus's *The Rebel: An Essay on Man in Revolt,* I've gained a new understanding of what it means to be a rebel. As Camus underlines, rebellion is often a positive force in the world. It sees past the mental boxes that obscure our vision, revealing new paths to take that will lead us out from the status quo. Rebellion is what gets human beings back on course whenever we've wandered off into the weeds and set up camp there (which we are so very prone to doing).

Camus also points out that the person who is a rebel is not the same as an outlaw. The Outlaw, he says, breaks the rules. She feels like a stranger in a strange land, and she lays claim to her "specialness" and aloneness as an excuse for going her own way, even when it hurts others. The Rebel, however, says Camus, is not a loner. Like the Outlaw, she too has felt like an alien in a land where she not only doesn't fit but where she doesn't *want* to fit—but she has stepped away from her sense of herself as solitary and unique in order to join together with others to bring change to the world, to make it a better place.

Joining together on behalf of others is essential to being a true rebel, one committed to standing up and speaking out for justice. Rebellion, insists Camus, "can only find its justification in human solidarity." He goes on to say, even more emphatically, "We have, then, the right to say that any rebellion which claims the right to deny or destroy this solidarity, loses simultaneously its right to be called rebellion and becomes in reality an acquiescence to murder."

In today's world, where partisanship has become nearly an insanity, these are good words to remember. As someone who practices Celtic spirituality, I am not interested in forming another denomination or faction, nor am I setting myself up as a spiritual Outlaw, intent on undermining perspectives that do not agree with my own. My devotion to Celtic spirituality shouldn't focus on my resentment against my past experiences with political parties, the church, or society in general, nor on complaining about current events. Resentment, according to Camus, is both divisive and passive. Rebellion is unifying and active.

Camus describes resentment as something that's sealed up and bottled, a creative force that is blocked from doing any good in the world. Rebellion, on the other hand, "breaks the seal and allows the whole being to come into play. It liberates stagnant waters and allows them to become a raging torrent." Rebellion, keeps us from getting bogged down in resentment, because true rebellion has nothing to do with

complaining about all the things we don't like in the world. Instead, it takes action. It takes a stand. Rebellion, says Camus, is a passionate affirmation of the integrity of all life.

As human beings we cannot function without a community of living relationships—but at the same time, we fail each other over and over. As individuals, we fail our children and our friends and our lovers; on a larger scale, our institutions (whether religious, political, educational, or societal) are prone to corruption.

We can become paralyzed by passive resentment at the individuals and organizations that have hurt us—or we can take a stand and speak out on behalf of compassion, forgiveness, and transformation. We can work together to liberate ourselves and our communities from our own mistakes and hypocrisies. Together we can become a raging torrent for good.

As we join our hearts and lives with the other rebels whose words have been included in this book, may we, as Camus insisted so vehemently, be inspired "to dedicate ourselves for the duration of our lives to the house we build—to the dignity of humankind and to the Earth—reaping a harvest that sows its seed and sustains the world again and again."

> *Do not wait for someone else to come and speak for you. It's you who can change the world.*
>
> —Malala Yousafzai

It is not enough to be compassionate. You must act. There are two aspects to action. One is to overcome the distortions and afflictions of your own mind, that is, in terms of calming and eventually dispelling anger.... The other is more social, more public. When something needs to be done in the world to rectify the wrongs, if one is really concerned with benefitting others, one needs to be engaged, involved.

—the Dalai Lama

V

THE INNER BATTLE

Marjory Bennet

> It is necessary to remember...
> that we all have the capacity to act
> in ways that oppress, dominate,
> wound (whether or not that power is
> institutionalized). It is necessary to
> remember that it is first the potential
> oppressor within that we must resist
> ...otherwise we cannot hope for an
> end to domination, for liberation.
>
> —bell hooks

This world's not going to change unless we're willing to change ourselves.

—Rigoberta Menchú

Somewhere along the way, as ideas about God and our relationship to the Divine One have evolved over the centuries, some of us picked up the idea that spiritual people are meant to be neutral in the world's many external conflicts, holding ourselves apart in a detached state of serenity. We assumed that if we sought to follow a spiritual path, especially one that focused on contemplation and mysticism, then we must exist on a higher plane than the issues that divide our world.

The Christian Celts of the early medieval period knew better (as have all the mystics, I suspect, from

Buddha to John Wesley, from the Dalai Lama to Lucretia Mott, and from Mother Teresa to Joan of Arc). They knew that true spirituality is a fierce and passionate fight to bring unity to the world—unity between humans and God, between humans and their neighbors, and most of all, unity within our own divided hearts.

Detachment is essential to a mystic path of spirituality, but when the mystics spoke of detachment, they did not mean we are to detach from the world in the sense that we no longer care about what's going on it. When we hear about injustice in our communities, we are not to meekly fold our hands and mouth pious platitudes about God's will. Instead, the challenge is to detach from our own egos—the selfishness within our hearts that insists that we come first, that we deserve to have our own way, that our lives matter more than others'—so that we are free to take action on behalf of justice.

This detachment allows us to act with clarity and humility, unencumbered by self-interest and pride. And this is the inner battle that the Celtic saints fought, a battle that must be fought daily for all of us who seek to follow a similar spiritual path. The ongoing interior struggle is the foundation of both our spirituality and our call to activism in the world. Without that inner battle, any external struggle in which we engage may easily become one more form of egoic activity, making us feel important, stroking our pride.

Ironically, even a "spiritual path," I've discovered, can turn into an ego trip. I suspect all forms of spirituality are vulnerable to this, but I can speak from experience for only two versions—conservative Evangelicalism and Celtic Paganism.

Growing up in a "fundamentalist" church, I was surrounded by what Beth Green refers to as an "ethic of resignation" in her 2016 blog post titled "The Spirituality of Activism & the End of Neutrality." As a teenager, I heard our minister blame the world's injustices on sin: AIDS was homosexuals' punishment; urban crime and poverty were also the consequences of sin; and when children starved in Africa, it was because their parents had refused to accept Christ as their personal Savior. As "born-again Christians" we might give lip service to feeling sad about these tragedies, but our pastor reminded us that we must "surrender to God's will."

Connected with this churchy apathy and resignation was also a sense of superiority. The congregation was certain that their version of Christianity was the right one, the *only* right one. Believing this so firmly, it made sense to them that saving souls from eternal hell (by convincing others to believe in our church doctrines) was far more urgent than saving physical bodies from earthly poverty, disease, and discrimination.

I became increasingly disillusioned with my religious background as I grew older, and eventually, I left it far behind me. In its place, I dove into Celtic Paganism, finding there a refreshing change from the religion of my childhood. In Paganism, I discovered a lovely, luminescent world filled with Divine meaning. I felt at home there in a way I never had in my fundamentalist church. Christian life had seemed to me to be narrow, rigid, and closed-minded. By contrast, Paganism was a wide, rich path that led me to a sense of wonder and vast, open possibilities.

Eventually, however, I could no longer avoid a suspicion that had been nibbling at the back of my mind: Wasn't I just as proud and self-righteous about my new spiritual path as the funamentalist Christians were about theirs? Wasn't I as certain that I was right and they were wrong as they were that they were right and I was wrong? Didn't I take as much egoic satisfaction in my mystical experiences of the Otherworld as Chrisitans did in their "answers to prayer"?

In article her blog post, Beth Green describes the modern-day religious paradigm she refers to as the "egoic version of spirituality":

> "I" am separate from you and my spiritual quest is separate and personal as well. In this paradigm, seeking my enlightenment, not revolutionizing

our world, is the hallmark of a spiritual life. God has created the world, and I can busily indulge myself in a spiritual quest for my own enlightenment, which allows me to overcome negative feelings about God's creation and float off in a haze of gratitude and acceptance. I don't change things. I accept them. . . . In this scenario, I do not have to be concerned with the well-being of the whole, either spiritually or materially, because I'm only seeking my enlightenment. This is self-indulgence in the name of God.

This attitude of spiritual self-indulgence would have made no sense to the passionate men and women who followed Jesus during the medieval Celtic era. Their pre-Christian forebears would not have comprehended this form of egoic "spirituality" either. Both Celtic Paganism and Celtic Christianity, in their ancient forms, viewed individual spirituality as an essential gift to the larger community as a whole.

The concept of focusing on one to the exclusion of the other (individual spiritual experiences over community life or community life over individual spirituality) would have seemed nonsensical. For them, one side of the equation fed the other in a continual circular flow. Their inner and outer realities were a unified whole.

In our dualistic understanding of the world (spiritual versus physical, internal versus external, self versus other), we have too often, as a society, failed to make this vital connection. This is what Carl Jung warned against when he wrote:

> Mastery of the inner world, with a relative contempt for the outer, must inevitably lead to great catastrophe. Mastery of the outer world, to the exclusion of the inner, delivers us over to the demonic forces . . . and keeps us barbaric despite all outward forms of culture.

In the ancient Celts, we find a practical template for avoiding this dichotomy.

One variation of this template is the Celtic concept of *awen*. Awen is both a modern-day Pagan notion and an ancient one that dates back to at least the eighth century (and probably far earlier). The Welsh word is often translated as "creative inspiration," but it has a much deeper meaning having to do with a transformed relationship between inner and outer reality. The person adept at awen was called an *awenydd*, someone who returned from her mystical experiences with down-to-earth patterns for harmonizing the entire community with the visible world as well as the invisible Otherworld.

Druids practiced extended times of solitude and silence when they engaged in a form of meditation called *dercad*, which enabled them to withdraw their minds completely from the sense-perceived world in order to become one with the Universe. This allowed them to imbibe awen from the Goddess's cauldron, radically transforming their perspectives on whatever problems they faced. The Druids emerged from dercad with useful insights for the entire community, as well as increased strength for their practical roles of service and leadership.

Author Kenneth McIntosh describes the practices of the early Celtic saints in a similar way, saying that they "oscillated between life-in-community and life-as-hermits." McIntosh goes on to say:

> Celtic faith has always had a strong activist element—believers wanted to transform society—and yet at the same time, they realized the limits of human strength. As a result, women and men seeking spiritual perfection adopted a wavelike rhythm for their lives, at times intensely engaged in teaching and acts of charity, while at other times withdrawing completely alone to desolate caves or

islands. In solitude, their souls were filled, so they could empty themselves in seasons of service—and then retreat again for refreshment.

Please note that I'm not advocating we fall into the error of idealizing and romanticizing the Celtic past (as those of us who are in love with Celtic mythology and spirituality are so prone to doing). All human beings (including the ancient Celts, both Pagan and Christian) are flawed and imperfect, susceptible to blinding ourselves to our own hypocrisy, prejudice, and selfishness. As a result, we are capable of espousing the noblest of ideas while treating each other with intolerance and downright cruelty. That is why the inner battle is so important, for without it, we inevitably become the mirror image of the very things we claim to oppose.

Renouncing our own egos is the essential element of this battle. And I want to be clear that I have known people who were far ahead of me in this struggle, people who were truly humble and selfless, who were both conservative Christians and Pagans. Just as no group can claim to have the corner on truth, no group should claim to have the corner on humility and compassion. Instead, let us learn what we can from each other, including those ancient Celts who have gone before us.

Describing the Desert Mothers and Fathers, who inspired the Celtic saints, Thomas Merton wrote that their spiritual paths led to "purity of heart—a clear unobstructed vision of the true state of affairs." It is this "clear unobstructed vision" of both our own hearts and the world around us that is so essential for any external activism, an activism rooted in, as Merton said, "an intuitive grasp of one's own inner reality as anchored, or rather lost, in God."

The Celtic connection between this world and the invisible world is a breathing, experiential reality, one that expands our inner selves at the same time that it ripples out into the outer world. As author Anthony

Duncan wrote, "The Celtic Saints were intuitives whose feet were very firmly planted on the ground." He went on to say, "It is their equilibrium as human beings which is much of their appeal, and in this, as in the holiness their lives display, they are Christlike."

Christlike. There's a word that's tossed around a lot in Christian circles. I know it means different things to different people, but for me, ultimately, it was Jesus Christ who brought me to a new understanding of my spiritual path. Because of him, today I call myself a Pagan follower of Jesus. For me, Jesus exemplifies the unity between the call to be actively involved in this world's struggles and the call to be actively engaged in the spiritual world. The Incarnation, God revealed in human flesh, is a challenge to live the spiritual life in fellowship with others—the "Body of Christ," the Incarnation as it's expressed in the Earth's global community.

Martin Luther King Jr. wrote that Jesus' life and death were "the eternal expression of the length to which God will go in order to restore broken community." According to King:

> The resurrection is the symbol of God's triumph over all the forces that seek to block community. The Holy Spirit is the continuing community-creating reality that moves through history. He who works against community is working against the whole of creation.

This is a spirituality that reaches across religions. One need not be a "Christian" to be "Christlike." In the words of John, "Everyone who loves has been born of God and knows God. Whoever does not love does not know God, because God is love" (1 John 4:7,8 NIV). It's that simple.

Love, therefore, becomes the hallmark of the activism that emerges from the endless war against ego and selfishness. Engaging in this interior struggle requires that we not only refuse to physically hurt our opponents but that we also refuse to hate them. It means that we don't seek to defeat or humiliate those who disagree with us, but instead we actively work to heal our shattered communities. In the words of Scripture, "If people say they love God but reject their fellow human beings, they are liars, for how can you love an invisible God if you are unable to love the visible human beings within your community?" (1John 4:20, my paraphrase of the Hebrew). Love overwhelms hate, creates reconciliation, and makes possible the creation of what King referred to as the "beloved community."

This is the true fruit of mysticism. As Quaker mystic Thomas Raymond Kelly wrote, when we enter in the "Eternal Presence," we find "our neighbors to right and left, before and behind," while the Divine "is over all and beneath all." This experience, wrote Kelly, "does not consist in achieving a mental state of concentrated isolation from one's fellows. But . . . it is as if we found our separate lives were all one life, within whom we live and move and have our being.

Beth Green writes of "spiritual activism," which asks that we not only "attempt to stop the behaviors of harmful individuals, corporations, the greedy or corrupt," but that we also acknowledge that those qualities exist everywhere, including our own hearts. Spirituality, says Green, calls us to heal our broken world, to restore oneness and harmony to what has been so hideously fractured.

This is the spiritual reality the ancient Celts understood, a flesh-and-blood experience of healthy relationship between all members of the community that is the result of a living unity of what we think of as the spiritual world and physical worlds.

"If we only blame," Green says, "we have betrayed Oneness itself." She continues:

> We must always be alert to our own desire to separate and to pander to our narrow interests and our prejudices. We must call out everyone on separation and discrimination, including

ourselves. . . . Spiritual activism is the fight for Oneness, and that inspiration is the guiding light of our lives. Love—practical, active work for the good of others—is the root of any true social activism. Love doesn't come easily to our selfish hearts, though. It requires that we engage in a constant fight against our own desires for power and control, a fight that's fought not only daily but moment by moment.

That's the reality that the ancient Celtic mystics, both Pagan and Christian, understood. From Myrddin, the Celtic shaman, to Columba, the Celtic saint, they fought against their own selfish passions (not always successfully), seeking to bring justice and harmony into visible reality within their communities. May we follow in their footsteps!

Beloved One, I pray that we may have the courage and integrity to follow the trail of bread crumbs the Celtic saints have left for us, endlessly resisting all that is selfish and egoic within our own hearts, so that we may persist as instruments of Divine Love,

> Change will only come about when each of us takes up the daily struggle ourselves to be more forgiving, compassionate, loving, and above all joyful
> in the knowledge that, by some miracle of grace, we can change as those around us can change too.
>
> —Mairead Corrigan Maguire

Peace...starts within each one of us.
When we have inner peace, we can
be at peace with those around us.
When our community is in a state of
peace, it can share that peace with
neighboring communities....
When we feel love and
kindness toward others, it not only
makes others feel loved and cared for,
but it helps us also to develop
inner happiness and peace.

—the Dalai Lama

VI

BUILDING A JUST SOCIETY

Lilly Weichberger & Kenneth McIntosh

> God places us in the world as fellow workers—agents of transfiguration. We work with God so that injustice is transfigured into justice, so there will be more compassion and caring, that there will be more laughter and joy, that there will be more togetherness in God's world.
>
> —Desmond Tutu

We have really got to create a culture in our world today where we recognize that every human life is sacred and precious.

—Mairead Corrigan Maguire

Come with us for a moment on an heart-journey through a world that existed a thousand years ago—the world of the pre-Christian Celts. Although we often like to romanticize the faraway past, this was a world in some ways much like our own, containing both compassion and cruelty, wisdom and ignorance.

Imagine that you are wanderer, cold and hungry and lost as a bitter winter night is falling. Then, as you make your way through the growing darkness, you see a glimmer of firelight shining through the trees. You walk a little faster, hope blooming in your heart, and you smell on the wind the scents of peat fire and cooking.

A cottage comes into view, warmth and light spilling out from its open door. A woman with fiery red hair steps into the doorway. Behind her, you see both a forge and a cooking pot. "Welcome," she says to you. "Come in. Be warmed. Fill your belly. Find peace of heart. There is room for you here."

This woman is the Goddess Brigid, the triune Goddess of the Hearth, Goddess of the Forge, and Goddess of Inspiration. Her living flame offers warmth, comfort, and a sense of home, at the same time that it brings creative inspiration and connection with the Divine. She represents the very flame of life that glows at the nexus of human interrelationship. From this focal point, Brigid spreads her compassion out into the world.

Much like Kuan Yin, the Buddhist goddess of mercy, Brigid is a powerful spiritual reminder of all that ties us together as human beings. Her hearth and forge and spirit-fire all call us to build a better world, a world that's built on justice and compassion rather than profit and greed.

The coming of Christianity to the Celtic world often either demonized the pre-Christian deities or relegated them to myth and fairy tales. Brigid, however, was an exception. Her influence was so deep and abiding that it could not be easily stamped out. Instead, she was woven into Celtic Christian tradition as Saint Brigid.

For Celtic Pagans, Brigid continues to demonstrate her great compassion for those who are in need. Meanwhile, Christians Celts find in Saint Brigid a strong woman who actively demonstrated her love of the poor. No one who came to her monastery, whether friend or enemy, king or beggar, was refused food, clothing, or shelter. Her icon portrays her holding a scroll, which bears these words:

To care for the poor,
To lighten everyone's burden,
To comfort the suffering.

This triplet summarizes Brigid's call to activism. In both her goddess and saint forms, she challenges us do more than march and protest for justice, but to also reach out with strong arms and skilled hands to actively build a world built on compassion.

The Welsh, with their Celtic love of the number three, expressed this notion in triads:

There are three things each very like the other: an old horse playing the harp, a pig in a silk dress, and a person who lacks compassion prating about her holiness.

Three marvelous deeds: to forgive a wrong done, to amend everything possible, and to refrain from injustice.

In three things a person may be like the Divine: justice, wisdom, and compassion.

Three who are loved by the Mighty Ones: the just person, the compassionate person, the person who gives to others without regret.

The understanding expressed in these ancient Celtic words was akin to the Jewish notion of "shalom," a word that means far more than its English translation as "peace." The Hebrew word is derived from a root denoting perfection or completeness— what author Walter Brueggemann refers to as a "vision of wholeness" in which people are joined not only to the Divine but to each other and to the entire Earth in a healthy, inclusive web of relationship. Shalom, says Brueggemann, points to the Divine Spirit who "is on the side of justice . . . concerned for the well-being of those who lack the power to secure it." Shalom represents a just world, where no one is excluded and everyone has what they need to grow and prosper, emotionally, physically, spiritually. This is the same sense of justice expressed through Brigid in all her forms.

According to the old stories, Saint Brigid may have been a Druid who continued to be a miracle-worker after she began following the Way of Jesus. Her compassion for others brought about miracles that not only gave people what they most needed but also created an abundance that demonstrated the immense generosity of the Divine. Her cow could endlessly produce milk; her flagon of ale could quench the thirst of a host of people; the bacon and butter in her kitchen multiplied to feed both beasts and humans; and when she needed mead to serve her guests, honey came out of a stone.

Like all miracles, Brigid's go beyond the events themselves and serve as signposts to deep Divine truth. They are not merely wonders or fanciful stories but instead convey something important about how we are meant to live in relationship with our fellow creatures on this Earth.

From a Christian perspective, Brigid reminds us that Christ asked his followers to care for others' physical needs. Justice is the natural outgrowth of compassionate relationships with others. We cannot consider ourselves to be Jesus' followers in the tradition of Brigid and other Celtic saints if we ignore people who are physically ill, imprisoned, or hungry.

Some of us may not encounter a hungry person face-to-face every day (though many of us do)—but we cannot say we hear Brigid's call to justice while we ignore the reality of physical hunger in our world. According to the World Health Organization, six million people die every year from hunger-related issues. That's the same as the number of deaths from the Holocaust, but this happens *every year*. An increase of compassion from those of us who live in the developed world could turn this terrible tide.

But to do any good, this has to be an active compassion, one that's willing to do the practical work of building a more just world. Brigid, who milked cows and churned butter, gave away coats and sheltered the unfortunate, points the way for us to do that.

As we mentioned earlier, the Goddess Brigid has three aspects. As the Goddess of Inspiration, she is the poet and priestess; as the Goddess of the Forge, she is the smith and patron of the arts; and as the Goddess of the Hearth, she is the guardian of the home. Her three-in-one nature demonstrates the way in which Divine inspiration, human creativity, and hard work are braided together to build our world.

Brigid also unites within her being another element of a just world: gender equality. As the Goddess of the Hearth, she fulfills what are traditionally considered women's roles: midwifery, healing, cooking, and tending the hearth and home. The Celts had no problem, however, combining this aspect of Brigid with her role as Mistress of the Forge, where she was often shown wearing a leather apron, tongs in one hand and a sword in the other. She is a testament to the egalitarian nature of Pagan Celtic society, where women were valued and respected not only as mothers, wives, and daughters, but also as warriors, queens, priestesses, and craftswomen. She is a role model who demonstrates to us a healthier, more just way of life.

Many modern-day Pagans are working to build the world that Brigid represents. Starhawk, for example, made a recent statement on her Facebook page, saying that we must turn away from passivity and "actively acknowledge that racism and patriarchy are deep, inherent, endemic forms of perpetual violence that infuse our society deeply, and will take much thought and work and courage to transform."

She goes on to say:

> And for those of you who have said, "I love your Pagan, spiritual stuff but I'm not sure I'm with you on this"—this IS my spiritual stuff. The

Goddess I embrace is both love and rage . . . who inspires our passion for justice, and sustains us through the long hard work to bring it about.

Expressing similar ideas, Pagan author and activist David Salisbury recently stated:

Social justice is crucial in my spiritual life to the point of being my spiritual life. I cannot separate the two. Any time I'm able to contribute to the movements I'm involved in, I do so as an offering to my gods and the spirit of the world. It's a holy act for me. I was originally taught that Paganism is all about relationships—to people, the gods, and the land we inhabit. I think social justice is important to our many traditions because it's about healing and strengthening the relationships between the three.

Another Pagan author and activist, T. Thorn Coyle, commented:

> As someone who experiences the sacred in all things, it is incumbent upon me to honor that to the best of my ability. Injustice causes a rift in the fabric of being. It is part of my work as a spiritual person to try to mend that rift, to help reweave the fabric of love.

As people following a Celtic spiritual path, whether Pagan or Christian, Brigid reminds us that we are each actively responsible for re-creating the world. With her, we burn with inspiration, discovering creative ways to spread love and light. With sweat and muscle, we do the everyday work necessary to forge a new reality. and we light the world with a compassion that welcomes and nurtures the entire planet.

Coyle summarizes this intersection of action, spiritual work, and justice, which Brigid symbolizes with such radiance:

> We forget. We forget we are connected. We think our states of disconnection are the only reality,

but the deeper reality exists in remembering that we are all alive together. When I scrub pots at the soup kitchen, or stand for people in Oakland who have been killed by police, or talk about the importance of the Voting Rights Act, or help send supplies to tornado victims, or organize a blood drive, or write about racism , I do all of this as a reminder to my soul: "You are part of this whole world, and it is of you."

> *The few rich are the cause of the many poor.*
>
> *—anonymous fifth-century Celtic philosopher*

> Love lights more fire
> than hate extinguishes.
>
> —Ella Wheeler Wilcox

VII

❖❖❖

FACING THE OPPOSITION

Bruce Epperly

Instead of hating the people you think are war-makers, hate the appetites and disorder in your own soul, which are the causes of war. If you love peace, then hate injustice, hate tyranny, hate greed—but hate these things in yourself, not in another.

—Thomas Merton

*If you want peace,
you don't talk to your friends.
You talk to your enemies.*

—Desmond Tutu

A tale from the North African Desert Parents—who played a vital role in shaping the spirituality of the Celtic saints— tells of an encounter between Abba Lot and Abba Joseph. I believe this ancient story can illuminate our current spiritual adventures.

One day Abba Lot went to see the venerable Abba Joseph to seek spiritual counsel. "Abba Joseph," he confessed, "as far as I can, I say my daily office, fast a little, pray and meditate, I live in peace, and as far as I can, I purify my thoughts. What else can I do?"

In response, his elder companion stood and stretched his hands towards heaven. His fingers blazed like ten lamps of fire, and he responded, "Why not become fire?"

Become fire! Burn brightly, giving light and warmth to the world! Illumine your neighborhood and enlighten the world! Like the Celtic saints of old, we too can be inspired by this ancient story from the Desert Parents, those passionate third-century followers of Christ. But how do we become fire in the modern world?

In the context of today's post-modern and pluralistic context, spiritual leaders, laypersons, and seekers alike need to become fire to claim their vocation as God's companions on an adventure in global transformation and healing. We need to experience the vital currents of divine energy, inspiration, and blessing in our professional, personal, and political lives. We need to become fiery—illuminating, warming, and guiding—in the quest to heal the Earth.

Perhaps, we are already on fire, bearing within us the energy and wisdom of the birthing of the universe,

and we don't yet know it! Jesus said, "You are the light of the world." Some five centuries earlier, Gautama the Buddha counseled, "Be lights unto yourselves."

We need God's light—and experiencing Divine light creates spiritual fire. I believe that we are called to "become fire," that is, to be passionate about our love of God, neighbor, and the world. I also believe that a fiery faith can transform our lives and bring beauty to the world. Yet if we are not careful, this same passion can lead to polarization, insult, objectification, and diminishment of others.

"Any great change must expect opposition, because it shakes the very foundation of privilege," wrote Lucretia Mott, the great nineteenth-century Quaker activist. How we choose to engage with the opposition we face can mean the difference between mirroring our opponents' attitudes from our own self-righteous positions of judgment—or bringing something altogether new and transformative to the conflict.

Accordingly, I have been pondering the counsel to "pray without ceasing" as a technique for engaging with what many of us think of as "the opposition." I have not always been successful at keeping my cool (especially in my Facebook interactions), but a spiritual attitude, grounded in prayerful intentionality, enables me to see the Divine in people with whom I disagree or whose positions are grounded in what I believe to be error. I choose to pray for politicians I oppose on the grounds of their ethics, character, and policy.

Because Facebook has become the mirror of our society, the place where many of us make our voices heard, I have come up with the following practices:

❖ Take a few deep centering breaths when I log on as a way of opening to a deeper wisdom and calm

❖ Pray for wisdom and inspiration in my conduct on Facebook.

- ❖ Pray to see the holiness in others, especially those with whom I disagree.

- ❖ Take a moment to reflect on my posts before I post them, mindfully asking myself the following questions:
  - Are these beneficial to those who read?
  - Are they inspired by ego or the quest for truth and reconciliation?
  - Am I attached to being right more than sharing the truth as I understand it?
  - Do I honor the holiness of the other?

- ❖ Take a moment to bless those individuals whose posts are troubling to me and ask that they experience wholeness and insight on God's terms, not my own.

- ❖ Remember the fallibility of my own position before posting.

I have found these to be good practices for every arena in which I interact with those who disagree with me. I still on occasion feel angry, anxious, and alienated. I suspect I will still make a few comments that don't bring out the best in others. But consciously turning my interactions over to Divine wisdom enables me to step back from my emotions. It allows me to speak out on behalf of justice with greater effectiveness.

Focusing on Facebook may seem like a small thing compared with all the other opportunities we have to engage in peace and justice efforts—and yet recent history has proven the power of social media to bring about change in our world. At the same time, we are often at our most careless when we post comments on social media. We feel free to denigrate others' intelligence and beliefs in a way that most of us wouldn't if we had to look those individuals in the face while insulting them.

Facebook and other forms of social media can be powerful vehicles for truth and justice—but we have to choose to use them to bring wholeness and not alienation to the world. The goal of our resistance is not to defeat our opponents but to defeat injustice. We can disagree, but we need to do so with a spirit of friendship and reconciliation, guided by the "better angels" that Abraham Lincoln spoke of.

Then, our use of Facebook can become sacramental, a sign of God's presence at work in our world, a platform from which we can work to bring the healing and reconciliation of God's shalom.

The Celtic saints and the Desert Parents would have been mystified by Facebook, as well as many of the other realities of our day. But when it comes to using every word and interaction to build God's Realm on Earth—that's something they understood!

Do not be too quick to assume your
enemy is a savage just because he
is your enemy. Perhaps he is your
enemy because he thinks you are
a savage.... And perhaps if he
believed you are capable of loving
him he wouldno longer
be your enemy.

—Thomas Merton

> *Surely, in the light of history, it is more intelligent to hope rather than to fear, to try rather than not to try. For one thing we know beyond all doubt: Nothing has ever been achieved by the person who says, "It can't be done."*
>
> —Eleanor Roosevelt

VIII

THE POWER OF HOPE

Meg Llewellyn

> Hope is being able to see
> that there is light
> despite all of the darkness.
>
> —Desmond Tutu

> *Hope doesn't come from calculating whether the good news is winning out over the bad. It's simply a choice to take action.*
>
> —Anna Lappé

In today's world, many of us are feeling as though our hopes have been trampled into the mud. It's hard to hope for anything now. The future looks dark, terrifying. To continue to hope seems like whistling in the dark. It almost seems safer, less risky, to abandon all hope, batten the hatches, and prepare for the worst. I understand those feelings all too well—but I'd like to offer an alternative. What if we who seek to be activists, working together to build a better world, thought of ourselves as pilgrims?

A pilgrim is someone who leaves behind all that is safe and familiar and travels long distances, searching out new lands. She does so not as a tourist but as a way to live out her faith in God, giving it tangible expression. As activists, we experience a similar calling. We too launch out from the status quo, venturing into unknown territory, not out of boredom or simple curiousity but because we are working to create a better world. Like pilgrims, we look to transform our interior faith into an exterior reality.

According to C. S. Lewis in *Pilgrim's Regress*, a pilgrim is a person who "travels hopefully." Again, we could say something similar about those who work for their communities' health and healing: *an activist is one who works hopefully for the future.* As people who seek to follow a spiritual path at the same time that we are actively engaged in bringing justice to the world, the concept of pilgrimage allows us to disengage from our societal concepts of success and failure, and discover new ways of thinking about our work.

For the Celtic saints, the act of pilgrimage was not so much about reaching a particular goal as it was about an ongoing spiritual process in which hope had a vital function. Hope plays an equivalent essential role in activism, giving us the steady equilibrium we need to persistently resist things as they are so that we can build something better.

If, however, our attention is so fixated on the end results we have in mind, we will become discouraged in the face of constant frustrations. We need instead to value the process itself, while hope becomes the motivating force that pulls us forward, despite setbacks and seeming failures. Hope is what gives value to our efforts, even when they seem to miss their mark.

This runs contrary to many of our current ideas about hope. An online thesaurus gives these words as synonyms for "hope": *desire, wish, daydream, pipedream, aspiration*, all of which describe a flimsy kind of hope, the sort that circumstances can tear to shreds. These words indicate that we've lost sight of hope as something active and muscular—something practical and down-to-earth that gives meaning to our work.

Other synonyms offered in the same online thesaurus are *optimism*, *ambition*, and *expectancy*—but true hope isn't the same as either positive thinking or a goal-oriented perspective. The hope that would have been familiar to the ancient Celtic pilgrims had nothing to do with the "Law of Attraction," which says that the Universe will send us whatever we focus our attention on. Celtic pilgrims traveled hopefully, but they placed no specific claims on the future. They committed themselves to the voyage without insisting on a particular outcome for their travels.

In Old English, *hopa* meant "confidence in the future," but it wasn't a cheery outlook that was immune to dark days. It wasn't even a glass-is-half-full mentality that hoped for the best. Instead, the ancient version of hope saw the empty half of the glass, and it knew that there was darkness all around—but it still believed that there were possibilities, even in the darkness. There was action to take that would lead to something better.

In a comparable way, the activist has confidence in the future, and he does whatever he can now to build a brighter tomorrow. Hope is a frame of mind that always looks forward, that doesn't waste time looking over its shoulder at the past, and it doesn't worry about what could have been—but at the same time it doesn't insist on its own way. It is open to the mystery of grace. It's willing to be surprised. This is a hope that makes the activist willing to be changed by his work, to be transformed along the way.

Celtic voyagers like the sixth-century Brendan the Navigator and Maeldune, the protagonist of an eighth-century Celtic tale, set out on their sea journeys with this same kind of energetic hope. They sailed out into the unknown, open to whatever they would discover, and they allowed themselves to be transformed by their journeys. Maeldune, who originally was seeking justice for his father's death, learned the power of forgiveness, and Brendan found both hardships and great marvels that brought new grace and strength, not only to him personally but to his entire community.

Brendan's and Maeldune's tales are forms of *immram*, Celtic sea journeys. The literal translation of the Gaelic word *immram*, is "rowing about," implying a kind of traveling that is far less goal-oriented than we may be comfortable with today. These journeys were never straight lines from point A to point B. Instead, the stories' heroes were willing to risk losing their way. At one point, Maeldune tells his men to put down the oars and let God direct their course with the wind. Maeldune, like the protagonists of other Celtic immram, is willing to surrender his control and submit to being lost.

These ancient stories are all forms of what Joseph Campbell called the "hero's journey"—the individual's search for new meaning, which benefits the entire community. According to Campbell, we each have our own hero's journey to make. Like Brendan and Maeldune, we are all called to venture out past our familiar boundaries, into new territories where we discover amazing treasures, learn new things, and return with insights that will change our larger community as much as ourselves.

For the ancient Celts, the sea was a liminal place, a place that was betwixt and between the visible world and the invisible world. By engaging in social activism, we too move into a liminal place that connects our spiritual beliefs with the physical world, a space where we enter a new reality that's infused with grace and mystery. It is a place where we lay claim on the miraculous potential of God's Kingdom.

During Maeldune's and Brendan's sea journeys, there were no lines between the visible and invisible worlds; the pilgrims crossed back and forth unknowingly between the worlds as they moved from island to island. They faced long periods of hunger and thirst—and despair—but eventually they always came to another stopping place where they were refreshed with new hope. As we work to build God's Kingdom on Earth, our experiences are much the same. We too must eventually accept that our work, no matter how well planned, seldom runs a straight A-to-B line from one goal to the next. Instead, we are often "at sea." As Barbara Hillers wrote in her article "Voyages Between Heaven and Hell: Navigating the Early Irish Immram Tales," as we work to build a better world, we don't find "an orderly progression toward a state of grace" but "an unpredictable, arbitrary zigzag course."

After the 2016 election, President Obama reminded us that history doesn't move in a straight line. "We zig and we zag," he said. We take a step forward, we take a step backward. Sometimes we rush forward, and we feel inspired by the wave of transformation—and other times, we seem to lose all the ground we gained. Sometimes we do both at the same time.

In the real world, there are no happily-ever-after endings. Even our greatest successes are inevitably followed by periods of anguish and disappointment. We require a confidence in the future even in our darkest moments—and the willingness to keep working hard in order to make progress. Hope keeps us striving for something that still lies ahead.

In Rebecca Solnit's book *Hope in the Dark,* she writes:

> Hope locates itself in the premises that we don't know what will happen and that in the spaciousness of uncertainty is room to act. When you recognize uncertainty, you recognize that you may be able to influence the outcomes—you alone or you in concert with a few dozen or several million others. Hope is an embrace of the unknown and the unknowable.

Solnit writes of our current world: "This is an extraordinary time full of vital, transformative movements that could not be foreseen. It's also a nightmarish time. Full engagement requires the ability to perceive both." Hope doesn't deny these realities. It gets busy and works with whatever's there.

We need to recognize the important triumphs that have been won, and then accept that these are only milestones. The fact that there is still so much work to be done doesn't negate the victories. When women got the right to vote, it was an important milestone—but it didn't mean that misogyny had been laid to rest forever. When slavery ended in the United States, it was an enormous victory of truth and justice—but racism continued to raise its ugly head. The Civil Rights Movement didn't end racism either—but it moved us significantly forward. More recently, marriage equality didn't put an end to homophobia—but it was another victory. As Solnit says, "A victory doesn't mean that everything is now going to be nice forever and we can therefore all go lounge around until the end of time."

That is the Christ-story as well. The birth of Jesus changed our reality—but it did not mean that everything became hunky-dory ever after. We know all too well that wasn't the case. It was a beginning, not an ending. After the Incarnation, Christ's true followers down through the centuries have had to work hard, to fight fiercely upstream against the tide of hatred and injustice (some of which was done in the name of Christ).

Howard Thurman, the great theologian, author, and activist, speaks of hope as a "growing edge":

> Look well to the growing edge! All around us worlds are dying and new worlds are being born; all around us life is dying and life is being born. The fruit ripens on the tree, the roots are silently at work in the darkness of the earth against a time when there shall be new leaves, fresh blossoms, green fruit. Such is the growing edge! It is the extra breath from the exhausted lung, the one more thing to try when all else has failed, the upward reach of life when weariness closes in upon all endeavor. This is the basis of hope in moments of despair, the incentive to carry on when times are out of joint. . . .

The "growing edge" is a concept the ancient Celts would have understood, for it speaks of that liminal place where Earth meets Heaven, and life is interwoven with death. It is a natural and living aspect of reality, one that is always there, balancing destruction and despair with the ever-renewing life force.

When we look back at the Celtic saints who lived their lives with such courage and hope, we may see their world through the rosy haze of romanticized mythology. What do they have to offer us, practically, we may wonder, when their world was so much simpler and safer than ours? But that question overlooks the reality of the ancient Celtic world, a world that was every bit as dangerous and politically complicated as our own is today in the twenty-first century.

Beginning at the end of the eighth century, for example, coping with terrorism became a recurrent, almost routine challenge for Celtic Christians, as Viking raiders plundered the British Isles' coasts and navigable rivers. The major targets were usually the monasteries; Vikings massacred tens of thousands of monks and nuns, as well as countless laypersons.

Despite this constant danger, Celtic Christians still faced the future with undaunted hope.

Centuries later, another Celtic Christian, C. S. Lewis, had a similar understanding of the meaning of hope. In his book *Surprised by Joy,* Lewis writes about a concept he refers to as *Sehnschucht.* The meaning of this German word is very similar to the Welsh word *hiraeth.* Neither can be translated adequately in English, but some scholars define both as a romantic and hopeless longing for that which is unobtainable, a longing that drives us to fantasies about an Otherworld where this world's ugliness is replaced by joy and loveliness.

For Lewis, however, Sehnschucht meant something a little different. Yes, he said, it is the "longing to be reunited with something in the universe from which we now feel cut off," but it is "not yet" rather than "never."

Lewis understood Sehnschucht as our sense that things in this world are not as they are meant to be—and our longing for Heaven is what drives us to work to improve our world in tangible and practical ways. According to Sean Connolly in *Inklings of Heaven*, Lewis's Sehnschucht is a form of hope that is "less like the rungs of a ladder which must be climbed in an ascent to a heaven *up there* (or, indeed, out there) and rather more like the scaffolding being put in place which allows heaven to be built in the here and now of daily existence."

Some modern Christians use the "End Times" as an excuse for avoiding social activism: since God will one day put all things right in Heaven, why should we bother ourselves to work for a better world in this life? Neither the ancient Celtic pilgrims nor C. S. Lewis would have understood this perspective. For them, hope is what inspires us to work to bring Heaven to Earth, here and now, rather than waiting for some distant utopia to come to fruition in Eternity.

Lewis described Sehnschucht as the feeling we have all had that something is wrong with the world in which we live—and as a result, we feel a sense of homesickness for a better world, a longing for the "far-off country." We are pilgrims, traveling to the Homeland that calls out to our hearts. At the same time, however, the Realm of Heaven is not an unobtainable land we can only reach at the end of our earthly journeys. Instead, our pilgrimage consists of building this Holy Realm in the world where we live now. Our "homesickness" is not sentimentality but rather something practical and vital that inspires us to set out on a voyage to build Heaven here.

We cannot control our journey any more than the ancient Celtic navigators could. We will experience times of great success and triumph, but we will also have moments of darkness and failure. We will wonder at times if all is lost.

"Hope," wrote Rebecca Solnit, "is the belief that what we do matters even though how and when it may matter, who and what it may impact, are not things we can know beforehand."

Or you might say that hope is the ship that carries activists forward, even through setbacks and disappointments, on the long journey toward justice. The roughest seas and the fiercest winds cannot sink this ship, for hope is buoyant, strong, and resilient. It carries us ever onward in the struggle to build the Realm of Heaven, here, now.

> *I will not allow my life's light to be determined by the darkness around me.*
>
> —Sojourner Truth

> Pit race against race, religion against religion, prejudice against prejudice.
> Divide and conquer!
> We must not let that happen here.
>
> —Eleanor Roosevelt

IX

WE'RE STRONGER TOGETHER

Marjorie Bennet

> We are way more powerful
> when we turn to each other
> and not on each other,
> when we celebrate our diversity,
> focus on our commonality,
> and together tear down
> the mighty walls of injustice.
>
> —Cynthia McKinney

> *When we are dreaming alone*
> *it is only a dream. When we are dreaming*
> *with others, it is the beginning of reality.*
>
> —Hélder Câmara

There's a small but stubborn piece of my soul that has always longed to be a hermit. I am perfectly happy with my own company for days on end; some of my most creative work and deepest thinking comes from the long, quiet days spent all alone. During these solitary times, the Divine One seems closer, Otherworldly experiences come more often, and I feel I am in a state of joyful equilibrium rather than the fretful frustration I so often feel in the company of other human beings.

Once upon a time, I had the sort of job that meant I was busy with people all day long. I gave talks to community groups, taught seminars, served on committees. I told myself that I was working hard in my professional life to improve the world, but truthfully, I spent much of the time feeling as though everything I did was a pointless waste. I was angry and resentful of the administrators who ran the show, scornful of my colleagues, and not very patient with the people I claimed to be helping. I was working alongside other people but without any real unity. My arrogance and impatience separated me from others and made me ineffectual.

Having my personal and professional lives shattered sent me scurrying to my own quasi-hermitage, a rundown cottage in a remote rural area. There, after long months alone, I began to see myself and my purpose differently. I came to realize that humility may be the essential ingredient to activism of any form. Without it, all my work for others had really been work for myself. My pride had undercut all my efforts.

Before I could act on that knowledge, however, I had to endure the crushing blow to my ego as I realized how far off track I'd gone. Alone, I could lick the wounds to my injured self-concept, and I hated to risk going out into the world again. Better to stay right where I was, I told myself, hidden away from any chance of embarrassment.

I wonder if Columba, that fiery Irish saint, felt much the same shame and self-disgust after he was banished to Scotland for starting a war over a book of Psalms. Was there a part of him that longed to spend the rest of his life praying in lonely places where he wouldn't ever again have the chance to hurt others with his quick temper and pride? Did he tell himself (as I did), "Oh, I'm far more useful to God when I'm alone. Without the challenge of other people's needs, I'm a more spiritual person. I pray better. I'm so much more serene and saintly"? I can't say for sure what Columba went through during the crisis in his life.

The old stories tell us only that his guilt drove him to use his banishment constructively, and he went on to build a great center of faith and learning on the island of Iona. In the process, he gained a widespread and long-lasting reputation for wisdom, holiness, and compassion.

I have no such ambitions anymore. But the truth is, I have no vocation as a hermit either. As a Pagan follower of Jesus, I feel his call to be actively involved, in my own small way, in making the Realm of Heaven visible on Earth. And that is work that cannot be done all alone. It would be senseless to even try, since Jesus made clear, with his stories about yeast and wedding feasts, fishing nets and seeds, that the Holy Realm is a place of vibrant, interconnected community.

I have come to know myself well enough, though, to know that times of retreat from the world's noise and chaos are necessary to my spiritual and emotional health. I've also learned that if I let it, my ego will run away with its own importance, no matter where I am or what I'm doing. I need to be careful to use my alone time for greater inner clarity, so that I can examine the places where I've let selfishness and pride run my life.

With greater awareness, I can then be content doing small things for others. I don't need to be the person at the front of the room anymore, and I don't need power or prestige. I can contribute instead to a larger work in ways I would have once considered trivial—listening when others speak and offering encouragement; providing food, a place to sleep, or transportation; lending my writing skills to those who have a message without the tools to express it. My goal is no longer to feel important or in charge but to contribute however and wherever I'm needed.

And yet when I'm out in the world, surrounded by voices and the constant presence of others, I always yearn for the isolated peace of my little cottage. I've come to accept that's just the way it has to be. I can't work in harmony with others without regular times alone—but those private interior times only bear fruit out in the noisy exterior world.

Columba and the other Celtic saints experienced this same inner conflict I do: the craving for contemplative solitude struggling against the call to a more visible, more physically engaged contribution to the well-being of others. When you read the old stories, you find these long-ago men and women retreating to lonely rocks in the middle of the ocean, hiding out in tiny reed huts in the wilderness, and sheltering alone in remote caves. Ultimately, however, few of them could ignore the call to active participation in their communities. No matter how secret their hermitages, somehow people always found them.

I can imagine how frustrated I would feel were I to wake up one morning, happily thinking I was all alone in my cottage, that tiny secret place where I feel as safe and sure of my own identity as a snail in its shell—only to find that a bunch of folks were waiting outside my door clamoring for me to emerge and talk to them! This was what happened again and again to those poor Celtic saints who yearned to be alone with God: the demands of other people constantly interrupted their solitude.

To ignore others' needs would be selfish—and yet hermit-time seems to have been the necessary foundation for many activists' lives, the soil from which their work grew. Without these times of solitude, they would have lacked the clarity and courage they needed for their struggle. A prime example is my personal hero, Jesus of Nazareth. Before he began his activism (speaking truth and justice to the society of his day), he spent forty days in the wilderness, alone except for wild animals (a detail from the Gospel account that I've always loved). He emerged from this time with a sure sense of who he was and what he needed to do.

Solitude in Nature has a long history of offering refuge to those who need to escape the societal world.

Celtic legends are full of such stories. Myrddin, for example, the great Celtic shaman, driven mad by guilt for the death of his friends in battle, fled to the forest, where he lived as a wild man of the woods for many years. A sixth-century Irish woman named Melangell escaped the sexism of her day and lived as a hermit in a remote Welsh valley; like Jesus, she was alone except for wild animals (especially hares). In the seventh-century, Winifred, another Celtic woman, wandered alone for many years (according to some versions of the legend), while she recovered from the trauma of sexual assault. All these wounded individuals found emotional and spiritual healing alone in Nature.

Stories like these are not unique to the Celtic mystics of yesteryear. In the 1960s, the author and monk Thomas Merton escaped his frustrations with communal monastic life by withdrawing to a hermitage. And about a decade later, in the 1970s, a depressed college dropout named Billy Barr retreated into the

Rocky Mountains where he lived alone for the next forty-some years.

All these stories are about people who couldn't cope—or didn't want to cope—with the so-called "real" world. They didn't *want* to work together with others! But their stories don't end there. When Myrddin was healed of his madness, he eventually returned to play an active role in the politics of his day (perhaps even, if you believe the legends, helping King Arthur to establish the Round Table). After Melangell had been alone with her rabbits for fifteen years, a Welsh prince stumbled across her hermitage and persuaded her to abandon her solitary life and create a religious community. According to legend, Winifred wandered through the wilds of Wales, down into Devon, and from there across the channel into Europe, eventually reaching as far as Rome; when she finally returned from her travels, she was convinced that women could be more effective (not to mention safer) living in community. At the Synod of Winifred, she persuaded the Celtic church that vocations from God didn't necessarily need to be lived out in remote hermitages, as had been the practice. Winifred went on to build two convents and became the abbess of one of them.

Jumping forward into the twentieth century, sickness pulled Thomas Merton out of his hermitage, and while he was in the hospital, he heard stories of protests, riots, and war; for the final years of his life, he wrote and spoke on behalf of peace, tolerance, and understanding,

traveling around the world and building new bridges between religious traditions. As for Billy Barr, his boredom during the long Colorado winters drove him to record the details of everything he observed outdoors, and eventually, scientists sought him out for this information. Barr's decades of notes—on such things as the first and last snows and the snow levels in between, when hibernating animals wake, and when the birds return to the mountains—became central to the scientific community's understanding of climate change. Barr still lives alone in the mountains, but today he is in regular communication with scientists around the world, contributing to the work of healing and protecting our planet.

Clearly, hermits have played important roles in our world—but only when they left their solitary hideyholes to work together with the larger, noisy, messy world out there. Because the reality is this: we truly *are* stronger together. Imagine if Jesus had never called disciples. Or if Buddha had never had followers. Or if the Celtic saints had never shared their wisdom with their friends, building communal centers of learning, faith, and art that not only helped keep culture alive through the Dark Ages but that also spread new ideas around the world and down through the centuries.

When I first read of the Celtic saints, I pictured stern, long-bearded religious fanatics standing alone on craggy mountaintops, their arms uplifted in prayer. The saints did have these moments, but as I've come to know them better, I've discovered that friendship was an essential part of Celtic spirituality. The anamchara—the soul friend—was so essential to each individual that a person was considered unable to function at full capacity without one. Following Jesus' example, his early Celtic followers often chose twelve friends to accompany them on their travels. Eventually, each of these chose their own twelve companions, creating an ever-widening web of connection and influence.

Their mission was often to build new faith communities in other lands. At first, I also imagined the

Celtic saints as fanatical celibates who retreated from the world into austere religious houses. I've learned, however, that early medieval monasteries and convents were very different from those that existed just a few centuries later. While some of the members of the communities were celibate, not all were, and in fact, entire families often lived there. These communities were more like busy villages—or perhaps college towns—that were united around living out in daily, ordinary life its members' love of God and others (as well as their love of learning and the arts). They were far stronger together than they would have been alone.

And so, despite the ongoing hankering I have for quiet lonesome places, I've come to accept that human life as a whole is communal. Our brains are neurologically structured to thrive in connection with other human beings. Yes, groups of humans create atrocity and war—but only groups of other humans working together, not individuals standing all alone, can put an end to those atrocities.

A single person alone will never accomplish as much as a group of people together. Martin Luther King Jr.'s power lay in his ability to activate a population, which is what kept the Civil Rights Movement alive after his death. On January 21, 2017, millions of women (as well as men) encouraged and empowered each other by marching in their hot-pink hats in cities around the world to speak out for justice, launching a movement that still continues. The Arab Spring became a dramatic and visible revolution that picked up momentum as it spread from nation to nation, gathering more and more followers—and while it may seem as though the Arab Spring has turned into the Arab Winter, remember that the anti-apartheid cause in South Africa faltered and stumbled and seemed to fail while activist Nelson Mandela spent twenty-seven years in prison . . . and yet in the end, the movement continued and the evils of apartheid came to an end.

When I look back at the history of social change, I see that amazing things happened whenever many voices rose above their differences and called out together for justice. As they pooled their various skills and resources, each contributing whatever bits and pieces they had to offer, together they became a powerful, single voice that helped raise awareness and influenced decision makers in government and elsewhere.

Some people marched and organized—and that was vital to their movement. Others wrote articles and books, and that was important too. Some people painted pictures; others collected scientific data. Some people cared for the sick, some fed the hungry, some welcomed immigrants with friendship and practical help. There are countless ways people have changed the world—and all were far more effective when they were done in unity with others who were working toward the same goals of justice for all.

Today, I think of my hermit times not as escapes from the world but rather as another way I can contribute to what is truly the larger world—the world of Heaven on Earth. The insights I discover alone become gifts I can share, and the self-awareness I find allows me to better work in union with others, rather than at cross-purposes. As Thomas Merton discovered, the fruit of solitude is "living in true relationship with oneself, God, others, and nature, free of the illusions of separateness."

And yes: *we are stronger together.* Together, we can work to infuse the ordinary visible world with the presence of Divine Love. Together—introverts and extroverts, hermits and agitators, visionaries and pragmatists—we can change the world.

> I always feel the movement is a sort of mosaic. Each of us puts in one little stone, and then you get a great mosaic at the end.
>
> —Alice Paul

> Our motto must continue to be perseverance. And ultimately I trust the Almighty will crown our efforts with success.
>
> —William Wilberforce

X

PERSIST!

Ellyn Sanna

What is needed for dramatic change is an accumulation of acts, adding, adding to, adding more, continuing. We know that it does not take everyone on Earth to bring justice and peace, but only a small, determined group who will not give up during the first, second, or hundredth gale.

—Clarissa Pinkola Estes

Nothing great is ever achieved without much enduring.

—Catherine of Siena

I'm not a fan of delayed gratification. I don't like to wait for results. When my hard work doesn't pay off in what I consider to be a reasonable amount of time, self-doubt swamps me. I decide my efforts must be worthless. I'm tempted to give up. Three women, however, have taught me important lessons about persevering, lessons that I draw from again and again whenever I'm discouraged.

None of these women thought of themselves as activists, but all of them were mothers, of one sort or another. They knew about taking care of the world; they knew how to use their hands and arms, their feet and legs to demonstrate love. They also knew that most things get done not because of one huge dramatic act but rather by many small, persistent actions, each alone so ordinary and seemingly trivial as to be barely noticeable.

The first of these women was my mother-in-law, a ferociously competent homemaker who intimidated me with her brisk efficiency. Her refrigerator was always full of fresh food, every surface in her house gleamed with cleanliness, and each meal she prepared was a work of art and tastiness. Meanwhile, I hated housework and cooking. My refrigerator was mostly filled with out-of-date bottles of salad dressing, soggy carrots, and refrigerator dishes containing leftovers so old that their contents were unrecognizable. My approach to homemaking consisted of exhausting marathon sessions of cleaning and baking, followed by weeks of accumulating dust, takeout containers, and dirty laundry.

As the years went by, my mother-in-law and I became good friends, despite our differences. One day, she said to me, "I have a secret, you know."

I wondered what hidden sin she was about to confess to me, but then she said, "Little by little. That's my secret. That's how I get things done." She went on to explain that she never made up her mind to clean her entire house; instead, she'd decide to wipe off one counter, and when that was done, feeling a warm glow of accomplishment, she would sweep the kitchen floor, then wipe the smears off the bathroom sink . . . and so on.

"Every job I do is so little that it doesn't bother me," she said. "It only takes me five or ten minutes to do each one. And then it's done, and I feel so good that I do one more little thing, and then another, and another. My whole life, ever since I was a girl, I've just done things little by little. It makes things so easy."

I will not pretend that today, thanks to my mother-in-law's wisdom, my house is as spotless and overflowing with good food as hers was. Truth is, I don't much like housework; I'd far rather be writing or editing, reading or researching. But whenever I feel overwhelmed and discouraged by a task I've set myself, I hear my mother-in-law's voice saying, "Little by little. That's how things get done."

It's good advice for those of us who want to build a better world. When I look around and see all the world's problems, I'm tempted to say, "It's too much. It's hopeless. There's nothing I can do to change things, so why should I even try?" But then I say to myself, "Little by little," and I look around for some small thing I can do. Maybe it's writing a letter or phoning a senator; maybe it's researching how to compost to cut down on the garbage my household contributes to the local landfill; it could be signing a petition, sharing an article on Facebook, or deciding to fill a bag with garbage every time I walk on the beach while on holiday.

As activist Ilyse Hogue said when she was working for MoveOn.org:

Social change is about what you choose to do everyday, how you interact with your neighbors, where you buy your groceries, who you're voting for, where you keep your money in the bank, what kind of car you're driving. . . . I think that is where it starts. . . . It's not what action you take, but it's taking action that makes the difference.

In other words: *Little by little,* just like my mother-in-law always said.

The second woman who taught me about perseverance was someone I got to know in the pages of a novel I edited a few years ago. Her name was Mother Sima, and she was a character in Kenneth McIntosh's young adult fantasy, *Magic Reversed.*

There are certain books whose characters linger in my heart and mind with as much vividness and life as any flesh-and-blood person I've known. *A Wrinkle in Time* by Madeleine L'Engle is one of those books, as is J. R. R. Tolkien's Lord of the Rings trilogy and Lloyd Alexander's Prydain series. *Magic Reversed* is another. As Ken McIntosh and I worked on his book together over the course of several months, I came to love his characters as they made their way across England, battling the *neamh mairbh* (a kind of Celtic zombie) the entire way.

Mother Sima, one of these brave companions, is a warrior nun, a monster-killer. She's also a plump little woman dressed in a voluminous cloak who faces danger with a cheerful matter-of-factness.

As she leads the others down into the bowels of the earth to face the Dark Lord, one of them asks her, "What's our plan?"

"A very simple one," Mother Sima answers "We take advantage of whatever God gives us as it comes along. I trust the way will be given one step at a time."

One step at a time becomes the phrase that Finn, the book's protagonist, clings to throughout the long days of danger and darkness. Overcoming the Dark Lord seems an impossible feat, and Finn is forced to accept that he is no mythic hero who can defeat evil in a dramatic show of courage and skill. Exhausted, terrified, confused, all he can do is take one more step . . . and then another. One step at a time, he and his companions travel mile after mile. One step at a time, the Dark Lord and his undead servants are defeated.

Set in the Celtic world of the Dark Ages, *Magic Reversed* is a historical fantasy, but like all the best fantasies, it offers real-life wisdom. Like Meg in *A Wrinkle in Time,* Frodo and his companions in the Lord of the Rings trilogy, and Taran and his friends in the Prydain books, Mother Sima and the other characters in *Magic Reversed* are true activists who fight against evil with all their strength. They show us that building a better world is slow work that requires a stubborn persistent courage. Ordinary little people doing ordinary little things over and over can change the world. As Lady Galadriel reminds the hobbits in

The Fellowship of the Ring, "Even the smallest person can change the course of history." That's the message we can learn from fantasies like Lord of the Rings and *Magic Reversed*.

And In moments of discouragement and despair, I hear Mother Sima's voice almost as clearly as I can the memory of my mother-in-law's. "One step at a time," Mother Sima says. "That's how we fight evil."

"Somehow," Finn realizes, "all our small actions added up to be enough."

Activist Anna Lappé has learned the same lesson in her real-world work for sustainable food systems. When asked whether one person can really make a difference when the challenges we face are so huge, she responded:

People often say they feel like just a "drop in the bucket," with the sense of futileness that the idea conveys. But it's probably more accurate to say people feel they're a drop in the desert—their drop dissipates before even touching ground. If you think about the idea of a bucket as a container that holds all of our drops, you'd sense how fast a bucket can fill and that—you never know—you could even be the one drop that pushes the water over the edge.

Environmental activist Vandana Shiva expresses the same sort of idea: "If you just do your little bit without thinking of the bigness of what you stand against . . . just that itself creates new potential."

How do we defeat evil? *One step at a time.*

The third woman who taught me about perseverance was my own mother. It's a lesson I learned from her late in her life, after she had Alzheimer's, through a tiny incident that seems trivial—and yet, hers was perhaps the most profound message of the three.

One day, after I had taken my mother shopping, she found a necklace lying on the pavement in the parking lot—a silver pendant made from the intertwined strands of Celtic knotwork, embedded in a tangled mass of chain. I plucked and poked at the solid knot the chain had formed, and then I gave up. "We'll never be able to untangle that," I told my mother.

But she proved me wrong. Over the next few days, she spent hour after hour working at the knotted chain, loosening it little by little. I wondered at her ability to stick with a task without becoming bored or frustrated—and then I realized why my mother was able to do what I would never have had the patience to achieve. At that stage of her disease, she no longer was aware of the passage of time.

She was not bored, because she had no sense of how many hours she had been making the same tiny motions with her fingers. She was not frustrated because she couldn't remember the thousand times those tiny motions had already failed. For her, there was only *this* moment, a timeless, boundless space as small as a breath and at the same time so vast it could contain an endless task.

On the third day after my mother found the necklace, after what I estimated to be nearly twenty hours of steady picking at the tiny knotted links, my mother gave a sigh of satisfaction and let the pendant dangle from the full length of the untangled chain. "There," she said. "That wasn't so hard."

I cannot claim to be able to experience the timeless persistence of my mother's Alzheimer-raddled brain. I don't even want to, since my work requires daily schedules and weekly deadlines; how could I keep track of all my responsibilities without a sense of time? But thanks to her, I've come to realize how much patience and frustration, persistence and discouragement have to do with our brain's perception of the passage of minutes and hours and days.

Because of her disease, my mother was living in a different reality—but I believe that reality was just as "real," in its own way, as mine. I suspect she was experiencing what the medieval mystic Meister Eckhart described when he wrote, "There exists only the present instant . . . a Now which always and without end is itself new. There is no yesterday nor any tomorrow, but only Now, as it was a thousand years ago and as it will be a thousand years hence."

The Celts, both Pagan and Christian, also had a sense of a larger reality lying beyond the boundary lines drawn by our ideas about time. This reality was the Otherworld, a place where bards and saints could slip between the hours and days and years, into timeless moments that made the passage of time irrelevant. A century could be as short as a single breath; a breath could last an eon. All events in the long history of the world were gathered together there in a perfect, endless *Now.*

Most of us, however, cannot step free from our brains' perception of time ticking along, nor do we want to, for the most part—and yet we can remind ourselves that in some sense, our brains perceive an illusion. There is another reality as well, an eternal realm where everything simply *is.* Each flower is blossoming, each knot is being undone, each evil is being put right; nothing is late, nothing is taking too long, there is no reason for discouragement or frustration.

This is the mind-set we need to cultivate as we work for justice. The work we do today may show no visible evidence of success, but that could be because the fruition of the seeds we plant at this stage in history will come much later, according to our human chronology.

I can't imagine what it would be like if the thread of time on which my perceptions are strung was to break, scattering my experiences like beads. I often thought that must be what my mother's memories were like—beads rolling around without any thread to keep them in order: apple trees simultaneously being planted, growing, and bearing fruit.

"How are you, Mama?" I'd say to her when I spoke to her on the phone, and she'd always give the same answer: "I'm confused." Without time's linear reference system to make sense of her life, of course she felt confused. That was part of the tragedy of her condition.

And yet in these days when standing up for justice has become so essential to our lives, whenever

I'm overwhelmed with disappointment and frustration I think of my mother's perspective. I remember that solid knot of chain and how little by little, my mother pulled out the tangles, and I gain new strength and courage to persist in my own work, no matter how small and useless my efforts may sometimes seems. I remind myself of what Julian of Norwich wrote: "We see with a double vision, things as they are now and things as they will be in Eternity, but God sees both perspectives united." I believe that the Realm of Heaven is whole and complete and full of light and joy, *now,* at the very same time as we work in darkness and despair to mend our broken world.

Alli Chagi-Starr, who calls herself a "creative change maker and alliance builder," has said that the proper perspective is necessary for successful activism, a perspective that is willing to wait . . . and to persist despite the lack of immediate rewards.

We need to realize that we are seed planters. We are going to probably die before we see all those seeds become trees, and it doesn't matter. You just have to keep planting and know that other people will come along and water those seeds and that those trees are for our children's children.

By resisting things as they are—and persisting in our work to build a better world—we answer the call to justice: *little by little, one step at a time, inhabiting both time and Eternity. . . .*

> It's the action, not the fruit of the action, that's important.... It may not be in your power, may not be in your time, that there'll be any fruit. But that doesn't mean you stop doing the right thing. You may never know what results come from your action. But if you do nothing, there will be no result.
>
> —Mahatma Gandhi

> If a house is burning, and bucket of water is thrown on the blaze and doesn't extinguish the fire, this doesn't mean that water won't put out fire.
> It means we need more water.
>
> —Dorothy Cotton

XII

WAYS TO GET INVOLVED

Be of good cheer. Do not think of today's failures, but of the success that may come tomorrow. You have set yourselves a difficult task, but you will succeed if you persevere; and you will find a joy in overcoming obstacles. Remember, no effort that we make to attain something beautiful is ever lost.

—Helen Keller

This could be our finest hour.
Never has the world needed our message more.
...Now is the time to risk everything.

—Ronald J. Sider

Financial contributions are an important way to answer the call to justice—but often we make the most difference when we allow our whole selves to become genuinely involved with the lives of others. This doesn't mean playing the lady bountiful or the magnanimous philanthropist to people you view as needier than you are. Instead, it means entering a genuine relationship, one that allows for the respectful give-and-take that exists between equals. Sometimes what people need most is to know that they too are needed!

Nor does answering the call to justice with dedicated action necessarily mean you have to connect with an organization. Instead, the first step is to look around your own family, social circle, and community, and see where there are needs to which you could respond. Maybe a young person in your extended family lacks the necessary resources for overcoming a disability; an elderly neighbor may need someone to help her get groceries or take care of basic home maintenance; or an immigrant family in your community could need help adapting to their new home. The need for compassionate justice is everywhere, and we can often do the most when we work close to home. As the saying goes, "Think globally, act locally."

However, there are also many wonderful organizations that allow us to work with others to address specific issues in a focused way, bringing all our separate skills and resources together into a single targeted effort. The list that follows is by no means complete; it's meant to simply give you a sampling of some of the various organizations out there, so you can see where you might be able to make a difference in a cause that speaks directly to your own heart. These organizations need financial support, but they may also need your involvement at a personal level.

Alturi
www.alturi.org

Alturi is an online information hub that was created to bring together a community to help improve the living conditions of LGBTI (lesbian, gay, bisexual, transgender, and intersex) people globally by educating the public, engaging partners and allies, and encouraging and facilitating support. Its website features news stories and content to draw in supporters, educate and engage them on issues, and compel them to get involved. It's meant to provide an outlet for effective, meaningful, and relevant advocacy that is easy and accessible for all. By listing causes and organizations working in this area, Alturi informs you of opportunities to make a difference at the local level for LGBTI people everywhere.

buildOn
www.buildon.org

BuildOn empowers urban youth to transform their neighborhoods and the world through intensive community service. Globally, buildOn constructs a new school every three days in some of the economically poorest countries around the world. It needs fund raisers, as well as people who are willing to do construction work to build schools.

Daily Action
dailyaction.org

When you sign up with Daily Action, you'll receive a text every morning that gives you a simple action to take, such as watching and sharing a video, texting a piece of news to five friends, or calling your senator, member of Congress, or another appropriate official about a single specific issue. To join the community, text the word DAILY to the number 228466 (A-C-T-I-O-N).

Ella Baker Center for Human Rights
www.ellabakercenter.org

Named after Ella Baker, a black hero of the Civil Rights Movement, this organization works with people of color and low-income to shift resources away from prisons and punishment, and toward opportunities that make our communities safe, healthy, and strong. It needs fund raisers, writers, and other volunteers.

Fairtrade
www.fairtrade.net

Fairtrade is an alternative approach to conventional trade based on partnerships between producers and traders, businesses and consumers. The international Fairtrade system represents the world's largest and most recognized fair-trade network. It is looking for people to get involved as consumers, sellers, researchers, writers, and campaigners.

Fashion Revolution
www.fashionrevolution.org

Fashion Revolution unites people and organizations to work together toward radically changing the way our clothes are sourced, produced, and consumed, so that our clothing is made in a safe, clean, and fair way. The folks at Fashion Revolution believe that collaborating across the whole value chain—from farmer to consumer—is the only way to transform the industry, and their mission is to bring everyone together to make that happen. Their site offers a range of ways you can get involved.

Global Fund for Women
www.globalfundforwomen.org

Global Fund for Women exists to support groups that work every day to win rights for women and girls. These groups are working to ensure women can own property, vote, run for office, get paid fair wages, and live free from violence, including domestic violence, sexual assault, and harmful practices such as female genital mutilation. It needs volunteers who will help them spread their message through social media.

Heifer International
www.heifer.org

Heifer works with farmers—mostly women—to empower those living in developing countries to achieve self-reliance. This organization allows you to give livestock to a family that needs it or to fund larger community-wide projects. The core of its model is "Passing on the Gift," which means families share the training they receive, and pass on the first female offspring of their livestock to another family. This extends the impact of the original gift, allowing a once impoverished family to become donors and full participants in improving their communities. Through Heifer International, you can give a hungry family the training they need to feed themselves and their children, give a young girl a chance at an education, or empower a woman to have a voice in her community.

The Hunger Project
www.thp.org

The Hunger Project's goal is a world where every woman, man, and child leads a healthy, fulfilling life of self-reliance and dignity. It works to end hunger and poverty by pioneering sustainable, grassroots, women-centered strategies and advocating for their widespread adoption in countries throughout the world.

Besides financial support, the organization needs fundraisers, as well as skilled volunteers who can design, research, and translate.

Kiva
www.kiva.org

Kiva's mission is to connect people through lending to alleviate poverty. By lending as little as $25 on Kiva, you can help a borrower start or grow a business, go to school, access clean energy, or realize her potential in some other way. For some recipients, the loans are a matter of survival, while for others, they provide the fuel for a lifelong ambition; 100 percent of every dollar you lend on Kiva goes to funding loans. Kiva also needs volunteers who can translate and/or edit loan applications.

More Than Scientists
www.morethanscientists.org

This organization believes there are a lot of ways you can join the community that's tackling climate change, from taking personal actions that limit your greenhouse gas emissions to the way you vote, from signing petitions to speaking with your elected officials. It believes in an all-of-the-above approach, and it offers a list of more than twenty organizations where you can get involved in this vital issue.

MoveOn
www.moveon.org

MoveOn is the largest independent, progressive organizing group in the United States. It combines rapid-response political campaigning with deep strategic analysis, rigorous data science and testing, and a culture of grassroots participation that allows the organization to quickly identify opportunities for progressive change and then mobilize millions of members to seize them. MoveOn members step up as leaders by using the MoveOn Petitions DIY organizing platform to create their own petitions and campaigns to drive social change.

National Network to End Domestic Violence
www.nnedv.org

The National Network to End Domestic Violence (NNEDV) is a social-change organization dedicated to creating a social, political, and economic environment in which violence against women no longer exists. NNEDV offers a range of programs and initiatives to address the complex causes and far-reaching consequences of domestic violence. Through cross-sector collaborations and corporate partnerships, it offers support to victims of domestic violence who are escaping abusive relationships and empowers survivors to build new lives. From training and technical assistance to innovative programs and strategic funding, NNEDV brings much-needed resources to local communities. At its national and regional meetings, members share information and ideas with NNEDV staff and with each other, working together to develop comprehensive solutions. The website offers a range of ways you can help, including donating your old cell phone.

National Network for Immigrant and Refugee Rights
www.nnirr.org

The National Network for Immigrant and Refugee Rights (NNIRR) works to defend and expand the rights of all immigrants and refugees, regardless of immigration status. The organization draws its membership from diverse immigrant communities, while it actively builds alliances with social and economic justice partners around the country. As part of a global movement for social and economic justice, NNIRR is committed to human rights as essential to securing healthy, safe, and peaceful lives for all. Go to the website to see how you can help.

One Green Planet
www.onegreenplanet.org

One Green Planet's goal is to help create a world where we eat delicious food and use products that provide us with maximum benefit while having a minimum impact on the planet. It does this by informing consumers about the downstream environmental impacts of their lifestyle habits and providing tools and resources that empower consumers to make better choices. It uses the power of online media, grassroots activism, and partnerships to shape people-, animal-, and planet-friendly policies.

Resist
www.resist.org

Resist is a foundation that supports people's movements for justice and liberation. It redistributes resources back to communities that are at the forefront of change, while amplifying their stories of building a better world. It gives out grants four times a year to support grassroots groups that are building movements for justice and liberation and resisting systemic oppression through cultural organizing, art-making, and resilience building. Go to the website to find out more.

Showing Up For Racial Justice (SURJ)
www.showingupforracialjustice.org

SURJ is a national network of groups and individuals organizing white people for racial justice. Through community organizing, mobilizing, and education, SURJ moves white people to act as part of a multiracial majority for justice. It works to connect people across the country while supporting and collaborating with local and national racial justice organizing efforts. With chapters all over the United States. SURJ provides a space to build relationships, skills, and political analysis to act for change.

Southern Poverty Law Center
www.splcenter.org

If you witness or are the victim of a hate crime, first, call the authorities—but you can also help the Southern Poverty Law Center monitor these incidents by submitting the details in a form on its website. You can use the hash tag #ReportHate to share the link to this form with others and call out hate crimes on social media. Southern Poverty Law Center's Hatewatch blog monitors and exposes the activities of the radical right with articles about the latest news and headlines regarding hate crimes and hate groups, as well as provides updates on the organization's pending law suits. This is not the kind of news that is fun to read, and the privileged among us can easily pretend it does not exist. But we have to push past feeling uncomfortable and get to the part where we ask ourselves what we can do to counter the message of hate. The Southern Poverty Law Center's website offers practical ways to make a difference.

As we find ways to work for justice, it's helpful to keep these points in mind:

❖ *We don't have to be perfect.*

None of us live perfectly consistent lifestyles. We may hate the meat industry—and yet we love a good hamburger. We want to protect the environment and reduce our carbon footprint—but we also love to travel and so we use many gallons of petroleum fuel flying and driving every year. We want to support workers in other countries—even though we still have favorite items of clothing that were not made under fair-trade conditions. The problems are complex, and both their causes and their results are woven through our daily lives. Even our activism efforts cannot be completely divorced from our corrupted systems; for example, going to a protest march requires driving (which creates greenhouse gases), and using a computer to spread the word through social medium means using a machine with built-in obsolescence made from rare-earth metals. Acknowledging this reality doesn't excuse us from working to live lives that are consistent with the call to justice. Think how enmeshed slavery was in the economy of its day. Or how deeply embedded were the laws restricting women's lives. Those things would never have changed without the courage and perseverance of people who did the best they could, picking at the knot of the problem, untangling it until it could be seen clearly enough to be eradicated.

❖ *We don't have to prove ourselves to anyone.*

When we first dip our toes in activism, we may feel intimidated by all the people out there who have been at it so much longer and know so much more about it than we do. But this isn't a contest. It's about everyone simply doing whatever they can wherever they can. Remember the story Jesus told about the widow's mite (Luke 21:1–4)!

❖ *We don't have to do it all by ourselves.*

Individual action is important but collective action is how we truly change the world—plus, when the problems are so enormous, we need the encouragement we get from working with others. According to blogger John Halstead,

> Whenever you start to despair about the effectiveness of your actions, it may be a sign that you are too focused on the level of individual choice. Take a step back and ask yourself how you can turn your individual action into a collective action. . . . Building community is one of the most important ways to fight against the status quo.

❖ *And finally, we don't have to have all the answers to respond to the call to justice.*

The problems we face are not simple, and they have no easy solutions. We must do whatever we can, even if the size and complexity of the problem seems overwhelming. Every time we resist our society's injustice—and persist in resisting—we help to build a better world.

How will you answer the call to justice?

> You do not need to know precisely what is happening, or exactly where it is all going. What you need is to recognize the possibilities and challenges offered by the present moment, and to embrace them with courage, faith and hope.
>
> —Thomas Merton

> A small group of determined
> and like-minded people can change
> the course of history.
>
> —Mahatma Gandhi

X

THE INSPIRATION OF OTHERS' LIVES

> What counts is not the mere fact
> that we have lived. It is what
> difference we have made to the lives
> of others that will determine
> the significance of the life we lead.
>
> —Nelson Mandela

Life is short. Do not forget about the most important things in our life, living for other people and doing good for them.

—Marcus Aurelius

The Celts' strong sense of community extended out beyond the local, visible neighborhood, reaching across geographical and temporal space. Brigid was said to have been an intimate friend of Mary the mother of Jesus; Columba could see that a far-distant friend was about to slip and fall; Patrick heard voices calling to him from Ireland when he was faraway in Europe; and Brendan the Navigator visited with Judas Iscariot. Both the Desert Fathers and Mothers, who had lived centuries earlier in Egypt and the mythological hero Fionn mac Cumhail were as real to the Celtic saints as their next-door neighbors. (Patrick is even said to have converted the nephew of Fionn mac Cumhail, one of the "big men" who stepped out from the mists of time and made Patrick's acquaintance.) When the Celts read in Scripture about the "great cloud of witnesses" (Hebrews 12:1) that watches our actions, they understood it literally, as a vital, animate reality that gave them courage and strength.

As we respond to the call of justice, we too can be heartened by those individuals, both past and current, who have already found ways to answer that same call. The people whose voices have been included in this book were not perfect; they were not always consistent in their words and actions; they made mistakes. While they committed their lives to justice for one group of people, they were sometimes blind to their prejudice toward another group. Where that's the case, let us not be disillusioned or use their weakness to excuse our own apathy and lack of action—but instead learn whatever we can from their lives, while we "shrug off anything that weighs us down, including the failures that so easily encircle us. Let us persist and persevere in the struggle that is set before us" (Hebrews 12:1).

Maya Angelou (1928–2014) was an American poet, memoirist, and civil rights activist. She published seven autobiographies, three books of essays, several books of poetry, and is credited with a list of plays, movies, and television shows that span more than fifty years. Her work made her a spokesperson for black people and women; she was one of the first black American women who publicly discussed their personal lives. According to literary scholar Hilton Als, black female writers before Maya had been marginalized to the point that they were unable to present themselves as central characters in the literature they wrote. Als said that Maya's book *I Know Why the Caged Bird Sings* marked one of the first times that a black autobiographer could, as he put it, "write about blackness from the inside, without apology or defense."

Throughout Maya's career, she received dozens of awards and more than fifty honorary degrees,

Kofi Annan (born 1938) was the Secretary-General of the United Nations between 1997 and 2006. He was awarded the Nobel Peace Prize for having revitalized the UN and for giving priority to human rights during his years in office. The Nobel Committee also recognized his commitment to the struggle against HIV in Africa and his opposition to international terrorism. He is the founder and chairman of the Kofi Annan Foundation, which seeks to mobilize political will to overcome threats to peace, economic development, and human rights.

Susan B. Anthony (1820–1906) was a pioneer crusader for the women's suffrage movement in the United States. Her work paved the way for the Nineteenth Amendment to the Constitution, which gave women the right to vote.

Susan grew up in a politically active family that worked to end slavery. She was inspired to fight for women's rights when she was denied the right to speak in public while campaigning against alcohol. She realized then that no one would take women in politics seriously unless they had the right to vote, and so, with activist Elizabeth Cady Stanton, she founded the National Woman Suffrage Association in 1869. Together, they created and produced *The Revolution*, a weekly publication that lobbied for women's rights, and edited three volumes of *History of Woman Suffrage*.

Susan was tireless in her efforts on behalf of women, giving speeches around the country to convince others to support a woman's right to vote. She even took matters into her own hands in 1872 when she voted in the presidential election illegally. (She was arrested and ended up being fined $100—but she never paid the fine!)

Women did not gain the right to vote until fourteen years after Susan's death. In recognition of her dedication and hard work, the US Treasury Department put her portrait on one-dollar coins in 1979, making her the first woman to be so honored.

Marcus Aurelius (121–180) was a Roman emperor. In the final decade of his life he wrote a series of personal philosophies intended only for himself, which were later published as *Meditations*, which is still read today. In it, he wrote: "Concentrate every minute . . . on doing what's in front of you with precise and genuine seriousness, tenderly, willingly, with justice."

He described his thoughts on social justice even more clearly in another passage: "You participate in a society by your existence. Then participate in its life through your actions—all your actions. Any action not directed toward a social end is a disturbance to your life, an obstacle to wholeness, a source of dissension. . . . A branch cut away from the branch beside it is simultaneously cut away from the whole tree. So too a human being separated from another is cut loose from the whole community. . . . People cut themselves off—through hatred, through rejection—and don't realize that they're cutting themselves off from the whole civic enterprise. . . . We can reattach ourselves and become once more components of the whole."

Walter Brueggemann (born 1933) is a biblical scholar and theologian who is widely considered one of the most influential scholars of the Hebrew scriptures. Using the Bible as his starting point, he argues that the Church must provide a counter-narrative to today's dominant forces of consumerism, militarism, and nationalism.

In an interview with *Image* magazine he explained his perspective on the gospel of Jesus as an activist manifesto against the injustice of a consumer society:

> As I see it, gospel faith always has two roles in the face of any totalizing truth. On the one hand, it has to criticize and expose totalizing truth as an idolatry that cannot keep its promise. That means that I believe that the church's task is to expose what I call "military consumerism" that can never make us safe and never make us happy, and we have to stay at that, because people's lives are being devoured. The other task of the church in the face of a totalizing ideology is to invite people to an alternative. That's very much what Jesus did in the totalizing world in

which he lived, and his call to "come follow me" was a call to embrace an alternative way of life. The church has to invite people to think about and experiment with the fact that neighborly relations, and not the pursuit of commodity, are the goal of our life. . . . There never was a time when it was easy and obvious. When the church is in the midst of this totalizing military consumerism, it's in a scary place to articulate an alternative, but that's what's been entrusted to us in the Bible and in the gospel of Jesus Christ.

He went on to connect social justice with the writings of the Hebrew scriptures, explaining that if a country does not treat its marginalized people with justice, it undermines its own national security:

> The argument that the prophets consistently make is that internal social disobedience towards the poor evokes external threat. The incredible thing that the prophets did was to imagine a connection between the internal state of society and the external reality of geopolitics. . . . If you believe in the rule of God and that

everything is connected, then the abuse of marginated persons and marginated communities in our society is going to evoke the hostility of marginated communities in other parts of the world.

Walter is an ordained United Church of Christ minister. He has authored hundreds of articles and over sixty books.

Hélder Câmara (1909–1999) was a Brazilian Catholic archbishop during the country's military regime. He was sometimes called the "Bishop of the Slums" because of his passionate advocacy on behalf of the urban poor. With other clerics also involved with Liberation Theology, he encouraged his nations's peasants to free themselves by studying the Gospels in small groups and initiating social change based on their readings. Nearly one hundred thousand of these small groups sprang up in Brazil, challenging the authorities on issues such as wages, control of land, sanitation, police repression, and human rights. In 1959, Hélder founded Banco da Providência in

Rio de Janeiro, a philanthropic organization to fight poverty and social injustice by helping poor people get loans.

Although today Hélder is being considered for sainthood, during his lifetime, particularly at home in Brazil, he was often criticized for his controversial views. In an interview with Italian journalist Oriana Fallaci, he insisted that he was not a Marxist, as he'd been accused, but said, "My socialism is special, its a socialism that respects the human person and goes back to the Gospels. My socialism it is justice." He also complained, "When I feed the poor they call me a saint. When I ask why so many people are poor they call me a communist."

Despite facing censure in Brazil, Hélder continued to work for the poor. He wrote in a poem:

> We must have no illusions
> We shall not walk on roses
> People will not throng to hear us and applaud
> and we shall not always be aware
> of divine protection
> If we are to be pilgrims for justice and peace
> we must expect the desert.

Hélder was known for his humility. He loved to say that he identified with the story of Jesus' Triumphant Entry into Jerusalem—but he saw himself not as Jesus in the story but rather as the donkey that Jesus was riding. (This story encouraged Mother Teresa to adapt Hélder's attitude to Indian conditions by thinking of herself as serving God as an old cow.) In Hélder's obituary, *Independent* journalist Sue Branford wrote, "I remember, above all, his gentleness and his concern for everything in the world around him, including its animals and plants" (which earned him the nickname of Saint Francis).

Hélder brought to Catholicism a new tolerance and compassion that contributed to some of the changes brought about during Vatican II. "In the Father's house," he said, "we shall meet Buddhists and Jews, Muslims and Protestants—even a few Catholics too, I dare say." He concluded, "We should be more humble about people who, even if they have never heard of the name of Jesus Christ, may well be more Christian than we are."

Joseph Campbell (1904–1987) was an American mythologist, who worked in comparative mythology and comparative religion. His work covers many aspects of the human experience, and activists have seen in his writings about the "hero's journey" parallels to the their work for justice.

According to Joseph, the adventure begins in the everyday world, when a herald calls the hero or heroine to action; this is the moment when the individual can no longer ignore or resist the call to justice and is drawn to take action. Mentors along the way then support and encourage the hero, as the quest continues; activists also take courage from those who are more experienced in the fight for justice. The heroine is tested as she faces ordeals and trials; activists face criticism from friends and family, as well as the authorities, and they may even endure violence and legal action. The way is fraught with danger, but in the end, the heroine or hero wins a new victory for the land; those who make the journey on the path toward social justice face enormous odds to create a society that respects and cares for all people—but their work is what saves the world.

Joseph Campbell's work also created spiritual and intellectual bridges between faith traditions. His ideas offer useful building blocks for a spirituality that is inclusive and tolerant, while at the same time deeply meaningful and challenging.

Albert Camus (1913–1960) was a French philosopher, author, and journalist. During World War II, he joined the French Resistance cell Combat, which published an underground newspaper of the same name. This group worked against the Nazis, and Albert became the paper's editor in 1943. When the Allies liberated Paris in 1944, he witnessed and reported the last of the fighting. Soon after, on August 6, 1945, he was one of the few French journalists to publicly express opposition and horror when the United States dropped atomic bombs on Japan. He resigned from *Combat* in 1947 when it became a commercial paper.

Throughout the 1950s, Albert devoted his efforts to human rights. In 1951, he published *The Rebel,* a philosophical analysis of rebellion and revolution. In 1953, he criticized Soviet methods to crush a workers' strike in East Berlin, and in 1956, he protested against similar events in Poland and the Soviet repression of the Hungarian revolution in October. He was consistent in his call for nonaggression in Algeria

As a pacifist, Albert resisted capital punishment anywhere in the world. He wrote an essay against capital punishment in collaboration with Arthur Koestler, the founder of the League Against Capital Punishment.

Albert won the Nobel Prize in Literature in 1957 "for his important literary production, which with clear-sighted earnestness illuminates the problems of the human conscience in our times." He died in a car accident at the age of forty-six, leaving behind a large body of influential work that included novels, essays, plays, nonfiction books, and short stories.

Catherine of Siena (1347–1380) was born in Siena, Italy, her mother's twenty-fifth child (although half of Catherine's brothers and sisters, including her twin sister, did not survive childhood). When Catherine's older sister died at sixteen, leaving her husband a widower, her parents proposed that he marry Catherine as a replacement. Catherine, who was a young teenager at the time, went on a hunger strike and cut her hair short to mar her appearance. Eventually, she persuaded her parents to allow her to remain single, something unheard of for a woman in medieval Italy.

Like the Celtic Saint Brigid, Catherine developed a habit of giving things away to those in need, including her family's food and clothing, much to their frustration. In her twenties, she began to actively work on behalf of the poor, sick, and imprisoned. When the plague struck Siena in 1374 and most people fled the city, she and her followers stayed to tend the ill and bury the dead.

After the crisis abated, she embarked on a letter-writing campaign to reform the Church and society. She took her complaints straight to the top, exhorting Pope Gregory XI to take action and address the political problems that were damaging the Church. Gregory was swayed by her persistence, but then, in 1378, the Great Schism split Christendom between two, and then three, popes. Catherine spent the last two years of her life in Rome, speaking out against the schism and working for the unity of the Church. She died of a stroke at the age of thirty-three (brought on, perhaps, by anorexia).

In 1970, Pope Paul VI named Catherine a Doctor of the Church, making her one of the first two women to be given this title (the other was Teresa of Avila), which recognizes contributions made to Catholic theology and doctrine. (Only two more women have been named Doctors of the Church since then.)

T Thorn Coyle (born 1965) is a Pagan author, teacher, and activist. She has worked with Buddhists, Christians, Muslims, Jews, and atheists on justice issues, working particularly to fight homelessness and the death penalty. A political and social justice activist since her teens, Thorn has worked at a San Francisco soup kitchen serving the homeless for more than twenty years. More recently she has worked to help families of those affected by police violence. Together with members of her Solar Cross Temple, and other groups such as Heathens United Against Racism and the Anti Police-Terror Project, she has worked with local families affected by police violence and brutality and has organized vigils, participated in protest marches and civil disobedience actions, and been active in raising funds for those affected by natural and human-made disasters.

The Dalai Lama (born 1935) is actually the fourteenth incarnation of the Dalai Lama. Born on a straw mat in a cowshed, he was one of sixteen children in a farmer's family in a remote part of Tibet. He supports the possibility that his next incarnation could be a woman.

The Dalai Lama has an appeal that straddles cultures and political systems, making him one of the most recognized and respected voices for peace and justice today. On January 22, 2018, he tweeted, "We have to cultivate a vision of a happier, more peaceful future and make the effort now to bring it about. This is no time for complacency, hope lies in the action we take."

Dorothy Day (1897–1980) was an activist who worked for social causes such as pacifism and women's suffrage through the prism of the Catholic Church. In 1917, she went on a hunger strike after being jailed for protesting in front of the White House as part of an effort to get women the right to vote. In 1933, she helped found *The Catholic Worker,* a newspaper that gave birth to the Catholic Worker Movement, which tackled issues of social justice. Dorothy also helped establish special homes to help those in need. She was arrested several times for her involvement in protests.

Currently being considered for sainthood, Dorothy's personal life was not always what the Church considered to be saintly. Her marriage failed after only a year. Twice, she became pregnant from her relationships with other men, and she terminated one of these pregnancies with an abortion.

Dorothy dedicated her life in service to her socialist and spiritual beliefs. The movement she created continues to thrive to this day, with more than two hundred Catholic Worker communities across the United States and another twenty-eight abroad. With her lifelong commitment to the poor and her unstinting devotion to active nonviolence, she helped fashion a new understanding of the gospel.

Frederick Douglass (c. 1818–1895) was a social reformer, abolitionist, orator, writer, and statesman. Born into slavery, when he was about twelve, the wife of his so-called "owner" taught him the alphabet, but under her husband's influence, she came to believe that education and slavery were incompatible and one day snatched a newspaper away from him. Undaunted, Frederick continued to secretly teach himself how to read and write. In his autobiography, he related how he learned to read from white children in the neighborhood, and by observing the writings of the men with whom he worked. He later often said, "Knowledge is the pathway from slavery to freedom." As Frederick began to read newspapers, pamphlets, political materials, and books of every description, this new realm of thought led him to question and condemn the institution of slavery.

After escaping from slavery, he became a national leader of the abolitionist movement, becoming famous for his eloquent antislavery writings and speeches. Northerners at the time found it hard to believe that such a great orator had once been a slave.

Frederick also actively supported women's suffrage, and he held several public offices. Throughout his life, he was a firm believer in the equality of all people, whether black, female, Native American, or recent immigrant. He was also a believer in dialogue and in making alliances across racial and ideological divides. When radical abolitionists, under the motto "No Union

With Slaveholders," criticized his willingness to dialogue with slave owners, he replied: "I would unite with anybody to do right and with nobody to do wrong."

In Roy Finkenbine's online biography of Frederick, he describes him as "the most influential African American of the nineteenth century," and goes on to say that Frederick "made a career of agitating the American conscience. He . . . understood that the struggle for emancipation and equality demanded forceful, persistent, and unyielding agitation." Less than a month before his death, when a young black man asked him for his advice, Frederick immediately replied, "Agitate! Agitate! Agitate!"

Shirin Ebadi (born 1947) is an Iranian lawyer, and human rights activist. She was one of the first female judges in Iran and was the first Iranian woman to achieve Chief Justice status. She, along with other women judges, was dismissed from that position after the Islamic Revolution in February 1979. She was made a clerk in the court she had once presided over, until she petitioned for early retirement. Shirin then set up private practice, and over the years since, she has taken on many controversial cases defending political dissidents; as a result she has been arrested numerous times. Shirin was awarded the 2003 Nobel Peace Prize for her work for human rights, in particular, the rights of women, children, and political prisoners in Iran. She is the first Muslim woman to receive the Nobel Peace Prize, and only the fifth Muslim to receive a Nobel Prize in any field.

In addition to being an internationally recognized advocate of human rights, Shirin has also established many non-governmental organizations in Iran, including the Million Signatures Campaign, which demanded an end to legal discrimination against women under Iranian law. She is also a university professor and students from outside Iran often take part in her human rights training courses. She has published more than seventy articles and thirteen books dedicated to various aspects of human rights.

Clarissa Pinkola Estes (born 1945) is a poet, Jungian psychoanalyst, post-trauma recovery specialist, and author. Her life demonstrates a different sort of activism.

As a post-trauma specialist, Clarissa began her work in the 1960s with World War I, World War II, Korean, and Vietnam War soldiers who were living with quadriplegia. She has worked with severely injured "cast-away" children as well as war veterans and their families. She taught prisoners writing, storytelling, and traditional medicine practices. Clarissa also works with women coping with childbearing loss, families of murder victims, and people at natural disaster sites. She served Columbine High School and its local community for three years after the 1999 massacre there, and she continues to work with 9-11 survivor families. As a practitioner and trainer in cross-cultural traditional medicine and practices, Clarissa served with Maya Angelou and Coretta Scott King as a board member of the Maya Angelou Minority Health Foundation (now called the Maya Angelou Center for Health Equity).

Clarissa is managing editor for *TheModeratevoice. com,* a news and political e-magazine where she writes on issues of culture, soul, and politics. She is also a columnist on issues of social justice, spirituality, and culture. She successfully helped to petition the Library of Congress, as well as worldwide psychoanalytic institutes, to use language that is respectful and appropriate for all ethnic and religious cultures.

Her foundation, the Estés' Guadalupe Foundation, has funded literacy projects, providing printed local folktales and health-care and hygiene information for people in their own language. These texts are then used for learning to read and write. Clarissa testifies before state and federal legislatures on welfare reform, education and school violence, child protection, mental health, environment, licensing of professionals, immigration, traditional medicine in public health, open records, and other quality of life issues.

Mahatma Gandhi (1869–1948) was the leader of India's nonviolent independence movement against British rule. As a boy, he was shy and so fearful that he slept with the lights on even as a teenager. When he was eighteen, his family sent him to study law in England, where he struggled with the cultural differences. Upon returning to India, he fought to gain his footing as a lawyer. In his first courtroom case, he was so nervous that when the time came to cross-examine a witness, he went blank and ran from the courtroom.

After failing to find work as a lawyer in India, he went to work in South Africa, where he was appalled by the discrimination and racial segregation Indian immigrants endured at the hands of the white authorities. During a train trip to Pretoria, South Africa, a white man objected to Gandhi's presence in the first-class railway compartment, although he had a ticket. Refusing to move to the back of the train, Gandhi was forcibly removed and thrown off the train at the next station. This act of civil disobedience awoke in him a determination to devote himself to fighting the "deep disease of color prejudice." He vowed that same night to "try, if possible, to root out the disease and suffer hardships in the process."

He formed the Natal Indian Congress in 1894 to fight discrimination. Then, in 1906, Gandhi organized his first mass civil-disobedience campaign, which he called *Satyagraha* ("truth and firmness"), in reaction to the South African government's restrictions on the rights of Indians, including its refusal to recognize Hindu marriages. During his time in South Africa, he was first given the title of "Mahatma," meaning "Great Soul."

When Gandhi returned to India, he became a leading figure in the home-rule movement. Calling for mass boycotts, he urged government officials to stop working for the British Crown, students to stop attending government schools, soldiers to leave their posts, and citizens to stop paying taxes and purchasing British goods. Rather than buy British-manufactured clothes, he began to use a portable spinning wheel to produce his own cloth, and the spinning wheel soon became a symbol of Indian independence and self-reliance. Gandhi assumed the leadership of the Indian National Congress and advocated a policy of nonviolence and noncooperation to achieve home rule.

In 1930, he organized the "Salt March" to protest the British government's monopoly on the salt industry. Wearing a homespun white shawl and carrying a walking stick, Gandhi set out with a few dozen followers. By the time he arrived at the Arabian Sea twenty-four days later the ranks of the marchers had swelled, and Gandhi broke the law by making salt from evaporated seawater. The Salt March sparked similar protests, and mass civil disobedience swept across India.

India gained its independence from England, only to find itself then immersed in violence between Hindus and Muslims. Gandhi toured riot-torn areas in an appeal for peace and fasted in an attempt to end the bloodshed. Some Hindus, however, increasingly viewed Gandhi as a traitor for expressing sympathy toward Muslims, and in 1948, a Hindu nationalist assassinated him.

Gandhi's influence continued, despite his death, and inspired human rights movements around the globe, including those of civil rights leader Martin Luther King Jr. in the United States and Nelson Mandela in South Africa.

bell hooks (born 1952) is an activist, educator, social critic, and writer. Her books examine the function of race and gender in today's culture. Born with the name Gloria Watkins, she chose "bell hooks" as her pseudonym, in tribute to her mother and great-grandmother. She decided not to capitalize her new name to place focus on her work rather than her name, on her ideas rather than her personality.

Bell was raised in a small, segregated town in rural Kentucky, "a world where folks were content to get by on a little." Her community, she said, turned the hardships created by racism into a source of strength. It helped give her a strong sense of self that allows her today to speak out against racism and sexism. Bell began writing poetry when she was a child.

After receiving a scholarship to Stanford University, she began *Ain't I a Woman* when she was only nineteen. The book was published in 1981 and became important in discussions of racism and sexism. Eleven years later, *Publishers Weekly* ranked it among the "twenty most influential women's books of the previous twenty years." *While Ain't I a Woman* made bell an important name in feminist debate, she felt her job as a teacher was her most important form of political resistance. Today, bell remains an important figure in the fight against racism and sexism.

Isaiah (eighth century BCE) was a Hebrew prophet during the time that the Jewish people were captives in Babylon. Traditionally considered to be the author of the Book of Isaiah in the Hebrew scriptures, many biblical scholars today believe that Isaiah himself was not the only author of the book. The passages most certainly written by the historic Isaiah consistently call for justice for his people, as he passionately demands social and personal reform. Some Bible scholars claim that Isaiah was a vegetarian and a pacifist, on the basis of passages in the Book of Isaiah that extol nonviolence and reverence for life. The Book of Isaiah is quoted many times by the writers of the Christian scriptures, and he continues to offer comfort and counsel to readers today.

Jeremiah (~650–570 BCE) was another Hebrew prophet, as well as a reformer and the author of the biblical book that bears his name. The era in which he lived was one of transition for the ancient Near East, and the small nation of Judah was caught in this political milieu, struggling to maintain its own identity. Jeremiah spoke out loudly against the social injustice that corrupted his society. He denounced his people for their religious hypocrisy and called on them to effect genuine ethical reform. In response to his outspokenness, Jeremiah was arrested and tried on a capital charge. He was acquitted but may have been forbidden to speak publicly after that. Instead, he had a scribe write his messages on a scroll, which was read by the religious authorities, as well as the government.

Throughout his life, Jeremiah was a courageous and persistent voice for social justice—and yet he also suffered inner doubts and conflicts. By nature he was shy and lacked confidence in his ability to express himself. Despite this, he spoke out bravely, working to counteract his people's despair and give them hope for the future. His life and writings had a lasting impact: both Jesus and the author of the Book of Hebrews in the Christian scriptures refer to Jeremiah's words, and people today are still inspired and heartened by his writing.

Melanie Joy (born 1966) is an animal rights activist, who is a Harvard-educated psychologist, a professor of psychology and sociology at the University of Massachusetts, Boston, and a celebrated speaker. She has written numerous articles on psychology, animal protection, and social justice, and she is the president of Beyond Carnism, a nonprofit advocacy group she founded in 2010. She has published two books, *Strategic Action for Animals* and *Why We Love Dogs, Eat Pigs, and Wear Cows*.

Helen Keller (1880–1968) overcame adversity to become one of the twentieth century's leading humanitarians. At the age of two, she was stricken by an illness that left her blind and deaf. Beginning in 1887, her teacher, Anne Sullivan, helped her make tremendous progress with her ability to communicate, and Helen went on to college, graduating in 1904.

After college, Helen set out to learn more about the world and how she could help improve the lives of others. She became a well-known celebrity and lecturer, sharing her experiences with audiences and working on behalf of others living with disabilities.

Helen tackled social and political issues, including women's suffrage, pacifism, and birth control. She testified before Congress, strongly advocating to improve the welfare of blind people. In 1915, along with renowned city planner George Kessler, she cofounded Helen Keller International to combat the causes and consequences of blindness and malnutrition. In 1920, she helped found the American Civil Liberties Union.

Helen worked with the American Federation for the Blind to raise awareness, money, and support for the blind. She also joined other organizations dedicated to helping those less fortunate, including the Permanent Blind War Relief Fund (later called the American Braille Press).

In 1946, Helen was appointed counselor of international relations for the American Foundation of Overseas Blind. Over the next eleven years, she traveled to thirty-five countries on five continents, including a 40,000-mile, five-month trek across Asia. Through her many speeches and appearances, she brought inspiration and encouragement to millions of people, and the story of her life continues to be a challenge to us all to use everything we have, no matter our limitations, to help others.

Robert Kennedy (1925–1968) was a politician who worked hard for civil rights. After he graduated from law school, Bobby joined the US Department of Justice's Criminal Division. In 1953, he became advisor to the Senate Subcommittee on Investigations under Senator Joseph McCarthy. Bobby left the position just six months later because he objected to McCarthy's unjust investigative tactics. In 1954, Bobby joined the

Senate's permanent Subcommittee on Investigations as chief counsel for the Democratic minority.

In a speech to South African students, he said:

> Each time a man stands up for an ideal, or acts to improve the lot of others, or strikes out against injustice, he sends forth a tiny ripple of hope, and crossing each other from a million different centers of energy and daring, those ripples build a current that can sweep down the mightiest walls of oppression and resistance.

In 1957, Bobby was appointed chief counsel to Senate Select Committee on Improper Activities in the Labor of Management Field, where he helped uncover the corruption of Teamsters union leader Jimmy Hoffa.

When JFK was elected, Bobby was made attorney general and became one of JFK's closest cabinet advisors. After his brother's assassination in 1963, Bobby resigned as attorney general and ran successfully for senator of New York. During his time in office he advocated for the poor and human rights and opposed racial discrimination and the escalation of involvement in the Vietnam War.

In 1968, Kennedy ran against Eugene McCarthy in the presidential election primaries. He won the nomination, but he was assassinated shortly after he gave his victory speech.

Martin Luther King Jr. (1929–1968) was a Baptist minister and activist who became the leader of the American Civil Rights Movement. Widely known as one of the greatest nonviolent activists in world history, King drew inspiration from both his Christian faith and the peaceful teachings of Mahatma Gandhi. While others in the Civil Rights Movement were advocating for freedom by any means necessary, including violence, Martin used the power of words and acts of nonviolent resistance (such as protests, grassroots organizing, and civil disobedience) to achieve seemingly impossible goals. During the not-quite thirteen years (until his assassination) during which he led the movement, black Americans made more genuine progress toward racial equality than had been achieved in the previous 350 years. He lead similar campaigns against poverty and international conflict, always maintaining his fidelity to his belief that all human beings everywhere are equal members of the human family.

Anna Lappé (born 1973) is an author, educator, and a sustainable food advocate. With her mother Frances Moore Lappé, Anna cofounded the Cambridge-based Small Planet Institute, an international network for research and popular education about the root causes of hunger and poverty. The Lappés are also cofounders of the Small Planet Fund, which has raised nearly $1 million for democratic social movements worldwide, two of which have won the Nobel Peace Prize.

Her project, Food MythBusters, is a collaborative project to break down myths about industrial agriculture and share the story of sustainable farming through creative movies, an online action center, and grassroots events. Food MythBusters is an initiative of the Real Food Media Project, which Anna directs, whose mission is to inspire, educate, and grow the movement for sustainable food and farming.

Anna's book, *Diet for a Hot Planet: The Climate Crisis at the End of Your Fork and What You Can Do*

About It, was named one of the best environmental book's of the year. Anna is also the coauthor of *Hope's Edge*, which chronicles social movements fighting hunger around the world, and *Grub: Ideas for an Urban Organic Kitchen*, showcasing the ecological and social benefits of sustainable food.

Mairead Corrigan Maguire (born 1944) is a peace activist who works with interfaith organizations and is a councilor with the International Peace Council. After three of her sister's children were killed during the violence between Catholics and Protestants in Northern Ireland, Mairead organized massive demonstrations and other actions calling for a nonviolent end to the conflict. Mairead was convinced that the most effective way to end the violence in Ireland was not through violence but through reeducation.

Along with Betty Williams, Mairead was the cofounder of Peace People, a movement committed to building a just and peaceful society in Northern Ireland. The two women organized peace rallies each week throughout Ireland and the UK for six months, which were attended by many thousands of people—mostly women—and during this time there was a 70 percent decrease in the rate of violence. The organization published a biweekly paper, *Peace by Peace*, and provided for families of prisoners a bus service to and from Belfast's jails. Mairead and Betty together won the Nobel Peace Prize in 1976.

Mairead has devoted her life to bearing witness to oppression and standing in solidarity with people living in conflict. Working with community groups and political and church leaders, she seeks to promote dialogue, nonviolence, and equality between deeply divided communities.

Nelson Mandela (1918–2013) was a South African revolutionary, politician, and philanthropist who was responsible for negotiating the end of apartheid in South Africa. After serving twenty-seven years in prison for his anti-apartheid activism, he was released in 1990, and then served as president of South Africa from 1994 to 1999. His lifetime of activism helped to bring peace to a racially divided country, and for the rest of his life, he continued to lead the fight for human rights around the world. He is said to have lived his life by three principles: free yourself, free others, and serve every day.

Thurgood Marshall (1908-1993) was a US Supreme Court justice and civil rights advocate. As legal counsel for the National Association for the Advancement of Colored People (NAACP), he guided the litigation that destroyed the legal underpinnings of Jim Crow segregation, and as an associate justice of the Supreme Court—and the nation's first black justice—he was an outspoken liberal on a Court dominated by conservatives. In his twenty-four year tenure, he voted to uphold gender and racial affirmative action policies in every case in which they were challenged. He also dissented in every case in which the Supreme Court failed to overturn a death sentence. According to the History Channel's website, "no other justice has been more egalitarian in terms of advancing a view of the Constitution that imposes positive duties on government to provide certain important benefits to people–education, legal services, access to courts–regardless of their ability to pay for them."

Cynthia McKinney (born 1955) is an American politician and activist who served six terms in the United States House of Representatives. Cynthia was active in the Civil Rights Movement from a young age, participating in numerous sit-ins and demonstrations as a teenager. She was the first black woman elected to represent Georgia in the House. Known for her fiery temper and controversial and outspoken stance on many issues, Cynthia has spoken out on various issues, including the rights of Hurricane Katrina victims and Palestinians.

Rigoberta Menchú (born 1959) is a Guatemalan indigenous-rights activist. Born into the Quiché Maya group, she spent her childhood helping with her family's agricultural work. As a young woman, she became an activist in the local women's rights movement and joined with the Catholic church to advocate for social reform. Her father was the leader of a peasant organization opposed to the government. The Menchú family's resistance efforts earned the negative attention of Guatemala's military government. During Guatemala's civil war, Rigoberta's father died in a fire while protesting human rights abuses by the military. Her younger brother was kidnapped, tortured, and killed by a military death squad in 1979, and her mother was kidnapped, raped, mutilated, and murdered by soldiers the following year. Rigoberta escaped to Mexico in 1981 and was cared for there by members of a liberal Roman Catholic group. She joined international efforts to make the Guatemalan government cease its brutal counterinsurgency campaigns against Indian peasants.

Rigoberta received the Nobel Peace Prize in 1992 for her continuing efforts to achieve social justice and mutual reconciliation in Guatemala; she used the prize money to found the Rigoberta Menchú Tum Foundation, an Indian advocacy organization. She also created the Indian-led political movement Winaq (Mayan for "the Wholeness of the Human Being") and began the legal process of creating a formal Winaq political party. If formed, it would be the first Guatemalan political party to directly represent indigenous groups.

Thomas Merton (1915–1968) was a Trappist monk who was also a pacifist and author. He took a nonviolent stance during the 1960s race riots and the Vietnam War, and he encouraged dialogue among people of different religions to achieve understanding. His books discussed his positions on social activism and Zen Buddhism and other faith traditions. He received praise from the Dalai Lama for his efforts to promote a greater understanding of East-West spirituality and teachings.

In 1968, while attending an interfaith conference in Bangkok, Thailand, Thomas stepped out of the bath and was electrocuted by an electric fan that had either short-circuited or had a break in the cord. His many books continue to be read, offering wisdom and guidance for the spiritual life.

Lucretia Mott (1793–1880) was a Quaker, abolitionist, women's rights activist, and social reformer. Determined to disengage herself and her household from the corrupt spiderweb of slavery, she (like many other Quakers of her day) refused to use cotton cloth, cane sugar, and other slavery-produced goods.

In 1821, Lucretia became a Quaker minister and traveled extensively, emphasizing in her sermons the "inward light"—the presence of the Divine—within every individual. In 1833, she helped found the American Anti-Slavery Society. Her speaking abilities made her an important abolitionist, feminist, and reformer. When slavery was outlawed in 1865, she advocated giving former slaves, whether male or female, the right to vote. "I have no idea of submitting tamely to injustice," she wrote. "I will oppose it with all the moral powers with which I am endowed. I am no advocate of passivity."

The issues of her day parallel many of our own, including the challenge for those who call themselves Christians to leave aside doctrine and focus instead on the real teachings of Christ. "The likeness we bear to Jesus is more essential than our notions of him," she said.

> It is time that Christians were judged more by their likeness to Christ than their notions of Christ. Were this sentiment generally admitted we should not see such tenacious adherence to what men deem the opinions and doctrines of Christ while at the same time in everyday practise is exhibited anything but a likeness to Christ.

Despite enduring constant digestive pain, Lucretia remained a central figure in the abolition and suffrage movement until the end of her long life. "Weep not for me," she said shortly before her death. "Rather let your tears flow for the sorrows of the multitude. My work is done. Like a ripe fruit I admit the gathering. Death has no terrors for it is a wise law of nature. I am ready whenever the summons may come."

Barack Obama (born 1961) was the forty-fourth President of the United States and the first black man to hold that position. Born in Hawaii, Barack was the child of a Kenyan father, of the Luo tribe, and an American mother, from Wichita, Kansas.

Barack attended Columbia University, where New York's racial tension made a deep impression on him. After graduation, he became a community organizer for a small Chicago church-based group, helping poor South Side residents cope with a wave of plant closings. He then attended Harvard Law School, where he became the first African-American editor of the *Harvard Law Review.* He turned down a prestigious judicial clerkship and instead practiced civil-rights law back in Chicago, representing victims of housing and employment discrimination and working on voting-rights legislation. He also began teaching at the University of Chicago Law School and married Michelle Robinson.

Barack then entered politics. He was elected to the Illinois state senate, then was elected to the US Senate as a Democrat, representing Illinois, and he gained national attention by giving a rousing keynote speech at the Democratic National Convention in Boston. During his years as a state senator, Barack worked to expand health-care services and early childhood education programs for the poor. He also created a state earned-income tax credit for the working poor.

In 2008, Barack ran for President and won. In his inaugural address, he called the nation to take action on such issues as climate change, health care, and marriage equality.

> We must act, knowing that our work will be imperfect. We must act, knowing that today's victories will be only partial and that it will be up to those who stand here in four years and forty years and four hundred years hence to

advance the timeless spirit once conferred to us in a spare Philadelphia hall.

He was reelected to a second term in November 2012. At his farewell address, as he left office in 2017, he said, "Change only happens when ordinary people get involved, and they get engaged, and they come together to demand it,"

George Orwell (1903–1950) was a novelist, essayist, and social critic. He was born Eric Arthur Blair, in Bengal, where his father was a minor British official in the Indian civil service. When he was older, George went to Burma, where he worked as assistant district superintendent in the Indian Imperial Police.

As he realized how much the Burmese resented British rule, George felt increasingly ashamed of his role as a colonial police officer. He decided to resign from the imperial police and immerse himself in the life of the poor and outcast people of Europe. Dressed in rags, he lived in the East End of London among labourers and beggars; he spent time in the slums of Paris and worked as a dishwasher in French hotels and restaurants; he tramped the roads of England with professional wanderers; and he joined the people of the London slums in their annual journey to work in the hop fields.

These experiences inspired his new career as a writer, while the revulsion he had come to feel toward imperialism led not only to his personal rejection of a privileged lifestyle but to a political reorientation as well. He changed his name from Eric Blair to George Orwell to represent this profound shift in his beliefs and the change in his identity from a pillar of the British imperial establishment into a literary and political rebel. Sometimes called the conscience of a generation, Orwell's best known novels, *Animal Farm* and *Nineteen Eighty-Four*, both speak to the dangers of totalitarianism and social injustice.

Rosa Parks (1913–2005) was a civil rights activist. When she refused to surrender her bus seat to a white passenger, her actions spurred on the Montgomery Bus Boycott that helped launch nationwide efforts to end segregation of public facilities. It was one of the largest and most successful mass movements against racial segregation in history.

Rosa's childhood had given her early experiences with racial discrimination. She had attended a segregated, one-room school that often lacked the most basic school supplies, such as desks. Black students were forced to walk to their schoolhouse, while the city provided bus transportation, as well as a new school building, for white students.

Throughout the rest of Rosa's education, she attended segregated schools, but in the eleventh grade, she had to leave school to take care of both her sick grandmother and her sick mother. Then, when Rosa was nineteen, she married Raymond Parks, a barber and an active member of the National Association for the Advancement of Colored People. With Raymond's support, Rosa earned her high school degree and she soon became actively involved in civil rights issues.

Although she had become a symbol of the Civil Rights Movement, Rosa suffered hardship in the months following her arrest in Montgomery. She lost her department store job, and her husband was fired after his boss forbade him to talk about his wife or their legal case. Unable to find work, they eventually left Montgomery and moved to Detroit, Michigan. There, Rosa made a new life for herself, working as a secretary and receptionist in US Representative John Conyer's congressional office. She also served on the board of the Planned Parenthood Federation of America.

In 1987, Rosa helped found the Rosa and Raymond Parks Institute for Self-Development. The organization runs "Pathways to Freedom" bus tours, introducing young people to important civil rights and Underground Railroad sites throughout the country.

Alice Paul (1885-1977) was a women's rights activist who was born into a prominent Quaker family in New Jersey. While attending a training school in England, she became active with the country's radical suffragists. Her education as an activist was expanded through a series of arrests, imprisonments, hunger strikes, and forced feedings. She learned how to generate publicity for the cause and how to capitalize on that publicity. After two years with the National American Woman Suffrage Association (NAWSA), she cofounded the Congressional Union and then formed the National Woman's party in 1916. Drawing on her experience in England, Alice led demonstrations and was subjected to imprisonment and beatings as she worked for a voting amendment for women. Eventually, her actions helped bring about the passage of the 19th Amendment in 1920. Alice continued to push for equal rights and worked with the National Woman's Party until her later years.

Eleanor Roosevelt (1884–1962) was a politician, diplomat, and activist. During her husband Franklin D. Roosevelt's four terms in office, she was a controversial First Lady because of her outspokenness on social issues, particularly her stance on racial discrimination. During her husband's presidency, Eleanor held regular press conferences, wrote a daily newspaper column and a monthly magazine column, hosted a weekly radio show, and spoke at a national party convention. On a few occasions, she publicly disagreed with her husband's policies.

Eleanor also broke with tradition by inviting hundreds of black American guests to the White House during her husband's years in office. When the black singer Marian Anderson was denied the use of Washington's Constitution Hall by the Daughters of the American Revolution, Eleanor resigned from the group in protest and helped arrange another concert on the steps of the Lincoln Memorial. Eleanor also arranged the appointment of black American educator Mary McLeod Bethune as Director of the Division of Negro Affairs of the National Youth Administration. Eleanor's support of black Americans' rights made her an unpopular figure among whites in the South but won her the support of blacks.

Following the Japanese attack on Pearl Harbor in 1941, Eleanor spoke out against Japanese American prejudice, warning against the "great hysteria against minority groups." She advocated for expanded roles for women in the workplace and the rights of World War II refugees.

After her husband's death in 1945, Eleanor remained active in politics for the remaining years of her life. She pressed the United States to join and support the United Nations and became its first delegate. She served as the first chair of the UN Commission on Human Rights and oversaw the drafting of the Universal Declaration of Human Rights. Later, she chaired the John F. Kennedy administration's Presidential Commission on the Status of Women. According to her obituary in the *New York Times*, by the time of her death, Eleanor was regarded as "one of the most esteemed women in the world."

David Salisbury is a Pagan author and activist. In a 2015 interview with Nimue Brown, he said, "Paganism is what began me on my journey as an activist. . . . In my paganism, I cannot ignore the troubles of the world because it is my responsibility as a nature-based faith member to help make the world a better place. Its the rent I pay to live on this planet. To me, a paganism without activism would feel hollow and disingenuous. Although I accept that not everyone will feel called to lead protests or lobby the government, I insist that we can all do something to contribute to justice and equality every day. Whether its learning about privilege, listening to oppressed communities, or volunteering. The Earth and her people demand that we do something. If nature-based faiths don't respond, who else can we depend on?" He is the author of *Wistchcraft Activism: A Toolkit for Magical Resistance (Includes Spells for Social Justice, Civil Rights, the Environment, and More)*.

Ronald J. Sider (born 1939) is a theologian and social activist. In 1968, Ron accepted an invitation from Messiah College to teach at its newly opened Philadelphia Campus in the inner city of Philadelphia. The racism, poverty, and evangelical indifference he observed at close hand there made a deep impression on him that led him to write *Rich Christians in an Age of Hunger.*

The injustice of the inner city also motivated him to work toward developing a biblical response to social injustice. He brought together a network of similarly concerned Evangelicals, which in 1973 became the Thanksgiving Workshop on Evangelical Social Concern, a think-tank that seeks to develop biblical solutions to social and economic problems through incubating programs that operate at the intersection of faith and social justice. Ron is also a founding board member of the National Religious Partnership for the Environment.

Starhawk (born Miriam Simos on June 17, 1951) is an American writer, teacher, and activist. In 2012, she was listed in Watkins' *Mind Body Spirit* magazine as one of the 100 Most Spiritually Influential

Living People. She believes that faith-based activism can reconnect us to basic human needs and that core religious values of community and self-sacrifice are important spiritually, as well as to the broader environmental justice movement. She advocates combining social justice issues with a Nature-based spirituality that begins with spending time in the natural world.

Starhawk's activism is also deeply rooted in an anti-war philosophy; she believes that war teaches us to see people culturally different from ourselves as inhuman and dangerous. She has written extensively on activism, including advice for activist organizers, examinations of white privilege within radical communities, and calls for an intersectionality of fighting oppression that includes spirituality, eco-consciousness, and sexual and gender liberation.

All of us have internalized an "oppressor," Starhawk argues, a "self-hater," and as a result oppression is a network that spreads out from each of us as individuals—but there is also the potential for liberation and healing to spread outward from each of us as well.

❖❖❖

Howard Thurman (1899–1981) was an author, philosopher, theologian, educator, and civil rights leader. As a prominent religious figure, he played a leading role in many social justice movements and organizations of the twentieth century. Howard's theology of radical nonviolence influenced and shaped a generation of civil rights activists, and he was a key mentor to leaders within the movement, including Martin Luther King Jr.

Howard traveled widely, heading Christian missions and meeting with world figures such as Mahatma Gandhi. He helped the Fellowship of Reconciliation establish the Church for the Fellowship of All Peoples in San Francisco, which was the first racially integrated, intercultural church in the United States. He became the Dean of Chapel at Boston University, making him the first black Dean of Chapel at a majority-white university or college in the United States. After leaving Boston University, he continued his ministry as chairman of the board and director of the Howard Thurman Educational Trust in San Francisco until his death.

Howard was a prolific author who wrote twenty books on theology, religion, and philosophy. The most famous of his works, *Jesus and the Disinherited*, deeply influenced Martin Luther King Jr. and other leaders, both black and white, of the Civil Rights Movement.

Krista Tippett (born 1960) is a journalist and author. She created and hosts the public radio program and podcast *On Being*.

At the beginning of her career as a journalist, Krista worked for the *New York Times, Newsweek,* the BBC, and other news agencies. She also became a special political assistant to the senior diplomat in West Berlin and then the chief aide in Berlin to the US ambassador to West Germany. She has said that moral questions arising from these experiences of seeing "high power, up close" eventually led to the spiritual, philosophical, and theological curiosity that has defined her work ever since.

Krista received a Masters of Divinity from Yale University in 1994 and began to think about how radio could be used as a vehicle for social change. She proposed a show about religion to Minnesota Public Radio in the late 1990s, and the program became a monthly series in 2001 and then a weekly national program distributed by American Public Media (APM).

In 2013, Krista left APM to cofound the nonprofit production company, Krista Tippett Public Productions, which she describes as "a social enterprise with a radio show at its heart." Krista is also the cocreator and convener of the Civil Conversations Project, which she has described as "an emergent approach to healing our fractured civic spaces."

Krista has shaped a style of radio interview that encourages dialogue between people from very different faith traditions. The *New York Times* said that her unique approach "represents a fusion of all her parts—the child of small-town church comfortable in the pews; the product of Yale Divinity School able to parse text in Greek and theology in German; and, perhaps most of all, the diplomat seeking to resolve social divisions." In 2014, Krista was awarded the 2013 National Humanities Medal at the White House for "thoughtfully delving into the mysteries of human existence."

Sojourner Truth (c. 1797–1883) was a women's rights and civil rights activist. She was born into slavery but escaped with her infant daughter to freedom in the North. She is best known for her speech on racial inequalities, "Ain't I a Woman?" which she delivered extemporaneously at the Ohio Women's Rights Convention. She devoted her life to the abolitionist cause and helped to recruit black troops for the Union Army.

Even in abolitionist circles, some of Sojourner's opinions were considered radical. She sought equality for all women and criticized the abolitionist community for failing to seek civil rights for black women as well as men. Although she began her career as an abolitionist, she worked for reform causes that were broad and varied, including prison reform, property rights, and universal suffrage.

Desmond Tutu (born 1931) is a South African Anglican archbishop known for his opposition to the policies of apartheid. Born in South Africa during apartheid, he understood as a child that he was treated worse than white children based on nothing other than the color of his skin. "We knew, yes, we were deprived," he said in an Academy of Achievement interview. "It wasn't the same thing for white kids, but it was as full a life as you could make it. I mean, we made toys for ourselves with wires, making cars, and you really were exploding with joy!" Desmond also recalled that one day when he was out walking with his mother, a white priest tipped his hat to her, which was the first time Desmond had ever seen a white man pay this respect to a black woman. The incident taught him that he need not accept discrimination and that religion could be a powerful tool for racial equality.

After Desmond graduated from high school, he was accepted into medical school, but his family could not afford the expensive tuition. Instead he accepted a scholarship to study education and graduated with his teacher's certificate. He then returned to his high school alma mater to teach English and history. "I tried to be what my teachers had been to me to these kids," he said,

> seeking to instill in them a pride, a pride in themselves. A pride in what they were doing. A pride that said they may define you as so and so. You aren't that. Make sure you prove them

wrong by becoming what the potential in you says you can become.

Desmond became increasingly upset about the racism corrupting all aspects of South African life under apartheid. The government spent one-tenth as much money on the education of a black student as on the education of a white one, and Desmond's classes were overcrowded. He decided he was no longer willing to participate in an educational system explicitly designed to promote inequality, and so he quit teaching—and enrolled in a theological college and was eventually ordained as an Anglican priest.

His rise to international prominence began when he became the first black person to be appointed the Anglican dean of Johannesburg. In this position he became one of the most powerful voices in the South African anti-apartheid movement. In 1984, he received the Nobel Peace Prize, which helped to transform the anti-apartheid movement into an international force with new supporters around the globe. The award also elevated Desmond to the status of a renowned world leader whose words immediately brought attention. Next, Desmond was appointed the Bishop of Johannesburg, and a year later he became the first black person to hold the highest position in the South African Anglican Church when he was chosen as the Archbishop of Cape Town.

His advocacy and leadership helped bring apartheid to an end. When Nelson Mandela became South Africa's first black president, Desmond was the one who formally introduced him to the nation. President Mandela also appointed Desmond to head the Truth and Reconciliation Commission, which was tasked with investigating and reporting the atrocities committed by both sides in the struggle over apartheid.

Although Desmond officially retired from public life in the late 1990s, he continues to advocate for social justice and equality around the world, focusing particularly on issues like treatment for tuberculosis, HIV/AIDS prevention, climate change, and the right for the terminally ill to die with dignity. In 2007, he joined the Elders, a group of seasoned world leaders that includes Nelson Mandela, Kofi Annan, Mary Robinson, Jimmy Carter, and others who meet to discuss ways to promote human rights and world peace.

Today, Desmond Tutu is known as one of the

world's foremost human rights activists. Like Nelson Mandela, Mahatma Gandhi, and Martin Luther King Jr., his teachings inspire all oppressed peoples' struggles for equality and freedom. "Despite all of the ghastliness in the world, human beings are made for goodness," he once said, expressing his optimism in the humanity's God-given potential.

Elie Wiesel (1928–2016) was a Nobel-Prize winning writer, teacher, and activist. Born in Romania, Elie pursued Jewish religious studies before his family was forced into Nazi death camps. Elie survived, but most of his family did not.

After the Allies released the death camp prisoners, Elie took up journalism, writing for French and Israeli publications. He wrote about his experiences in the camp in *Night* and went on to write many more books, while also becoming an international activist, speaking out against injustices perpetrated around the world, including South Africa, Bosnia, Cambodia, and Rwanda. He and his wife founded the Elie Wiesel Foundation for Humanity to "combat indifference, intolerance and injustice" throughout the world.

Elie won the Nobel Peace Prize in 1986. The Nobel citation honoring him stated:

> Wiesel is a messenger to mankind. His message is one of peace, atonement and human dignity. His belief that the forces fighting evil in the world can be victorious is a hard-won belief.

William Wilberforce (1759–1833) was a politician, philanthropist, and a leader of the movement to end the slave trade. He was born into a prosperous English merchant family, but with no interest in the family business, he decided to pursue a career in politics and became a member of the House of Commons. He was more interested in socializing and partying, however, than he was in any particular political issue.

The following year, William converted to Christianity, and everything changed for him. Questioning whether he should withdraw from politics, he consulted John Newton, the former slave trader who wrote the hymn "Amazing Grace." Newton encouraged William to continue in politics, believing that God could use him "for the good of the nation."

William began political work for humanitarian reform, and soon after, he was asked to bring the topic of the slave trade to Parliament. A growing body of people had been working to raise public awareness of the evil of slavery, but they were battling an economy that was deeply interwoven with the slave trade. William carefully reviewed the information and then did his own research. William collected statistics on the slave trade that included evidence of mistreatment and mortality rates. Confronted with the evidence of inhumane treatment and the high death rate on the slaves' sea passages, he became convinced that slavery was "so enormous, so dreadful, so irremediable in its wickedness that . . . from this time I determined that I would never rest till I had effected its abolition."

When the parliamentary debate began in 1789, many voiced opposition, fearing that Britain would be economically disadvantaged if the slave trade were outlawed. Others lacked sympathy because of the commonly held belief in the divine placement of one race of people over others. Slave traders painted a rosy picture of the slaves' circumstances at sea and argued that the high death rates were simply due to epidemics. William dealt with each argument presented and appealed to the members of Parliament to think beyond a short-term economic perspective and to view their responsibility from an eternal perspective. The debate was adjourned for nine days and ultimately delayed by a further two years. It was not until 1792, after William's opponents inserted the word "gradual" into the proposal, that the House voted that the slave trade should eventually be abolished.

Meanwhile, William devoted himself to many other social causes, including the education of the poor, prison reform, and paying the debts of those in debtors' prisons. He noticed that the Christianity found in the Bible contrasted sharply with the accepted religious practice of the day, and in response wrote *A Practical View of the Prevailing Religious System of Professed Christians, in the Higher and Middle Classes in This Country, Contrasted with Real Christianity*, which went on to be published in five languages.

Finally, in 1807, Parliament abolished the slave trade. Tears ran down William's face when he heard the decision, but he knew his work was not done. He began pushing for the liberation of all slaves and helped to form the Anti-Slavery Society. When poor health forced him to retire from politics, he sent a message to the Anti-Slavery Society: "Our motto must continue to be perseverance. And ultimately I trust the Almighty will crown our efforts with success."

What had once seemed impossible, came to be, thanks in large part to William's commitment to resist and persist. Three days before he died, the act for the abolition of slavery passed in the House of Commons, and the following year, slavery was abolished throughout Britain.

Ella Wheeler Wilcox (1850–1919) was an author and poet. She was a popular poet, rather than a literary one, but she used her words to express her concern for animal rights, disarmament, and social justice, as well as the many emotions of ordinary life. She was a believer in spiritualism and theosophy, and her works, filled with positive thinking, were popular in the New Thought Movement. She considered this life to be a "preparatory room," which is "only one of the innumerable mansions in our Father's house."

Malala Yousafzai (born 1997) is a Pakistani activist for female education and the youngest Nobel Prize laureate. Her human rights advocacy has grown into an international movement.

When she was a child, Malala's family ran a chain of schools in Pakistan. When she was eleven, she wrote a blog under a pseudonym for the BBC Urdu, describing her life during the Taliban occupation. The following summer, a *New York Times* documentary was made about her life, and as a result, she became well known around the world, giving interviews in print and on television. Desmond Tutu nominated her for the International Children's Peace Prize.

In retaliation for Malala's activism, a Taliban gunman attempted to murder her. Although she was not killed, she was seriously injured. The murder attempt sparked a national and international outpouring of support for her.

After her recovery, Malala became a prominent education activist. She founded the Malala Fund, a nonprofit organization based in Birmingham in the UK, and her book *I Am Malala* became an international best seller. In 2014, when she was only seventeen years old, she was awarded the Nobel Peace Prize for her struggle against the suppression of children and young people and for the right of all children to education.

> It's the action, not the fruit of the action, that's important.... It may not be in your power, may not be in your time, that there'll be any fruit. But that doesn't mean you stop doing the right thing. You may never know what results come from your action. But if you do nothing, there will be no result.
>
> —Mahatma Gandhi

READING NOTES

HOW TO READ THIS BOOK

For a wider background on Celtic history and spirituality, read Water from an *Ancient Well: Celtic Spirituality for Modern Life* by Kenneth McIntosh (Anamchara Books).

Audre Lorde's book *Sister Outsider* (Crossing Press) is a collection of fifteen essays and speeches that challenge sexism, racism, ageism, homophobia, and class. Audre is unflinchingly honest, but ultimately, she offers us a message of hope.

INTRODUCTION

To find out more about Anamchara Books' ideas about Celtic spirituality, check us out on Facebook or on our website, www.AnamcharaBooks.com.

Alexis de Toqueville published *Democracy in America* in 1835 and a second volume in 1840. In his book, he attempted to capture the essence of American culture and values. As a Frenchman traveling through the United States, he was able to write a clear-eyed and objective description of America's strengths and weaknesses, including its racism. He warned that American democracy had the potential to create new forms of tyranny because radical equality could lead to materialism and the selfishness of individualism.

Anna Julia Cooper. *The Voice of Anna Julia Cooper* (Rowman & Littlefield, 1998, reprint), p. 194. Dr. Anna Julia Haywood Cooper (1858–1964) was an American author, educator, sociologist, speaker, activist, and one of the most prominent African-American scholars in United States history.

The *Carmina Gadelica* is a compendium of prayers, hymns, charms, incantations, blessings, poems, songs, proverbs, and anecdotes gathered from ordinary people living in Scotland between 1860 and 1909. The material was recorded and translated from Gaelic into English by Alexander Carmichael (1832–1912).

Krista Tippett. *Becoming Wise: An Inquiry into the Mystery and Art of Living* (Penguin, 2016), p. 1.

Chapter I

Gera, Deborah (1997). *Warrior Women: The Anonymous Tractatus De Mulieribus* (E.J. Brill, Leiden, the Netherlands),

p. 10–11. The *Tractatus de Mulieribus* is a short ancient Greek work by an anonymous author that describes fourteen ancient women. It was written near the end of the second or the beginning of the first century BCE.

In *Ancient Laws of Ireland* (1894), editor Laurence Ginnell was one of the first scholars to note the similarities between the Brehon Laws and the Manu Laws of India.

Janet Tanner has a good article on the Penitentials: "The Irish Penitentials and Contemporary Celtic Christianity," *The Way*, 48/2 (April 2009), 63–78.

Columbanus: Studies on the Latin Writings, Volume 17 of Studies in Celtic History, Michael Lapidge, editor (Boydell & Brewer, 1997), p. 107.

"Pelagius on the Christian Life," in *Celtic Spirituality*, Oliver Davies & Thomas O'Loughlin, editors (Paulist Press, 1999), p. 402.

Chapter II

Read more about Brigid in Meg Llewellyn's book, *Celtic Miracles and Wonders: Tales from the Ancient Saints* (Anamchara Books, 2017), pp. 51–80.

L. M. Browning. *Seasons of Contemplation: A Book of Midnight Meditations* (Homebound Publications, 2015).

Elie Wiesel. *Messengers of God: A True Story of Angelic Presence and the Return to the Age of Miracles* (Simon & Schuster, 1985), p. 57.

Chapter III

Sierra Lomuto. "White Nationalism and the Ethics of Medieval Studies," *In the Middle*, December 5, 2016, http://www.inthemedievalmiddle.com/2016/12/white-nationalism-and-ethics-of.html.

Maev Kennedy. "African origin of Roman York's rich lady with the ivory bangle," *The Guardian*, 26 Feb. 2010, https://www.theguardian.com/science/2010/feb/26/roman-york-skeleton.

Roxanne Khamsi, "Genes reveal West African heritage of white Brits," *New Scientist,* 4 Jan. 2007, https://www.newscientist.com/article/dn11018-genes-reveal-west-african-heritage-of-white-brits/#ixzz64EW07E27.

Chapter IV

Albert Camus. *The Rebel: An Essay on Man in Revolt* (Vintage, 1992, reprint).

Chapter V

Beth Green. "The Spirituality of Activism and the End of Neutrality," *Daily Kos*, 27 Apr. 2016, https://www.dailykos.

com/stories/2016/4/27/1520750/-The-Spirituality-of-Activism-the-End-of-Neutrality.

Carl Jung. *The Secret of the Golden Flower: A Chinese Book of Life* (Houghton Mifflin, 1962), p. viii.

Kenneth McIntosh. *Water from an Ancient Well: Celtic Spirituality for Modern Life* (Anamchara Books, 2011), p. 218.

Thomas Merton. *The Wisdom of the Desert: Sayings from the Desert Fathers of the Fourth Century* (New Directions, 1970), p. 8.

Martin Luther King, Jr. *Nonviolence & Racial Justice* (Quaker Press, 2008), p. 9.

The Spirit of the Quakers (Yale University Press, 2010).

Chapter VI

Read more about Brigid in Lilly Weichberger and Kenneth McIntosh's *Brigid's Mantle: A Celtic Dialogue Between Pagan and Christian* (Anamchara Books, 2016).

Walter Brueggemann. *Living Toward a Vision: Biblical Reflections on Shalom* (United Church Press, 1982), p. 11.

Quotes from Starhawk, David Salisbury, and T Thorn Coyle can be found in Crystal Blanton's article "Social Justice as Spiritual Work in Paganism," *The Wild Hunt*, 16 Aug. 2013, https://wildhunt.org/2013/08/social-justice-as-spiritual-work-in-paganism.html.

Chapter VII

The Desert Fathers, Helen Waddell, trans. (Vintage, 1998, reprint).

Lucretia Mott is quoted in *Joyous Greetings: The First International Women's Movement 1830–1860* by Bonnie S. Anderson (Oxford University Press ,2000), p. 6.

Chapter VIII

C. S. Lewis. *Pilgrim's Regress* (Eerdmans, 2014, reprint), p. 31.

Read more about both Brendan and Maeldune in Meg Llewellyn's book, *Celtic Miracles and Wonders: Tales from the Ancient Saints* (Anamchara Books, 2017).

Barbara Hillers. "Voyages Between Heaven and Hell: Navigating the Early Irish Immram Tales," *Proceedings of the Harvard Celtic Colloquium,* vol. 13 (1993), pp. 66–81.

Rebecca Solnit. *Hope in the Dark: Untold Histories, Wild Possibilities* (Haymarket Books, 2016), p. xiv.

Howard Thurman. *Meditations of the Heart* (Beacon Press, 2014), p. 134.

C. S. Lewis. *Surprised by Joy* (Houghton Mifflin Harcourt, 1956).

Chapter IX

Read more about Columba in Kenneth McIntosh's *Water from an Ancient Well: Celtic Spirituality for Modern Life* (Anamchara Books, 2011).

Melangell's story is found in *Collections Historical & Archaeological Relating to Montgomeryshire and Its Borders*, Volume 34 (1907).

Robert of Shrewsbury (1484) tells the story of Saint Winifred.

Michael Mott has written the authorized biography of Thomas Merton, *The Seven Mountains of Thomas Merton* (Harvest Books, 1993).

J. Weston Phippen. "The Hermit Who Inadvertently Shaped Climate-Change Science," *The Atlantic*, 12 Jan. 2017.

Chapter X

Kenneth McIntosh. *Magic Reversed* (Anamchara Books/Candlewood, 2016).

Anna Lappé and Alli Chagi-Starr were interviewed by Britt Bravo, *The Mindful Word* 2012, https://www.themindfulword.org/2012/everyday-activism-change-world.

Vandana Shiva was interviewed by *Yes!* executive editor Sarah van Gelder, Winter 2012.

Meister Eckhart is quoted in Igor Kononenko's *Teachers of Wisdom* (Dorrance, 2010).

WAYS TO GET INVOLVED

John Halstead. "4 Things Every Aspiring Environmental Activist Should Know," *Patheos* 17 Sept. 2015, https://www.patheos.com/blogs/allergicpagan/2015/09/17/4-things-every-aspiring-environmental-activist-should-know/.

Additional Sources for Quotations

Angelou, Maya. *I Know Why the Caged Bird Sings.* New York, NY: Random House, 2009.

———. *Letter to My Daughter.* New York, NY: Random House, 2009.

Annan, Kofi. *Kofi Annan: A Spokeperson's Memoir.* Beijing: Ruder Finn, 2013.

Câmara, Hélder. *Dom Helder Camara: Essential Writings.* Ossining, NY: Orbis, 2009.

———. *The Desert Is Fertile.* Eugene, OR: Wipf & Stock. 2005.

Camus, Albert. *The Rebel: An Essay on Man in Revolt.* New

York, NY: Vintage, 1956.

Dalai Lama. *An Appeal to the World: The Way to Peace in a Time of Division*. New York, NY: William Morrow, 2017.

Duncan, Ronald, ed., trans. *Selected Writings of Mahatma Gandhi*. Boston: Beacon Press, 1951

Ebadi, Shirin. *Until We Are Free: My Fight for Human Rights in Iran*. New York, NY: Random House, 2016.

Eliot, T. S. *Selected Prose of T. S. Eliot*. New York, NY: Harvest Books, 1975.

———. *The Waste Land*. New York, NY: Colombia University Press, 2001.

Ellsberg, Robert, ed. *Dorothy Day: Selected Writings; By Little and by Little*. Ossining, NY: Orbis, 2005.

Estes, Clarissa Pinkola. *The Faithful Gardener: A Wise Tale About That Which Can Never Die*. New York, NY: HarperOne, 1995.

Joy, Melanie. *Strategic Action for Animals: A Handbook on Strategic Movement Building, Organizing, and Activism for Animal Liberation*. New York, NY: Lantern Books, 2008.

Keller, Helen. *The World I Live In and Optimism: A Collection of Essays*. Mineola, NY: Dover, 2012.

Kennedy, Robert Jr., ed. *RFK: His Words for Our Times.* New York, NY: William Morrow, 2018.

King, Martin Luther Jr. *The Essential Martin Luther King, Jr.: "I Have a Dream" and Other Great Writings.* New York, NY: Beacon Press, 2013.

Lappé, Anna. *Diet for a Hot Planet: The Climate Crisis at the End of Your Fork and What You Can Do About It.* London: Bloomsbury, 2011

Maguire, Mairead Corrigan. *The Vision of Peace: Faith and Hope in Northern Ireland.* Eugene, OR: Wipf & Stock, 2010.

McKinney, Cynthia. *Ain't Nothing Like Freedom.* Atlanta, GA: Clarity Press, 2014.

McKivigan, John R. and Heather L. Kaufman, eds. *In the Words of Frederick Douglass: Quotations from Liberty's Champion.* Ithaca, NY & London: Cornell University Press, 2012.

Menchú, Rigoberta. *I, Rigoberta Menchú: An Indian Woman in Guatemala.* London: Verso, 2010.

Merton, Thomas. *Conjectures of a Guilty Bystander.* New York, NY: Image, 2009.

Metaxas, Eric. *Amazing Grace: William Wilberforce and the Heroic Campaign to End Slavery.* San Francisco, CA:

HarperOne, 2007

Obama, Barack. *The Audacity of Hope: Thoughts on Reclaiming the American Dream*. New York, NY: Crown, 2006.

O'Driscoll, Mary, ed. *Catherine of Siena: Passion for the Truth—Compassion for Humanity*. Hyde Park, NY: New City Press, 2005.

Orwell, George. *Why I Write*. New York, NY: Penguin, 2005.

Painter, Nell Irvin. *Sojourner Truth: A Life, A Symbol*. New York, NY: Norton, 1997

Parks, Rosa. *Quiet Strength: The Faith, the Hope, and the Heart of a Woman Who Changed a Nation*. Grand Rapids, MI: Zondervan, 1994.

Quindlen, Anna. *Thinking Out Loud: On the Personal, the Political, the Public and the Private*. New York, NY: Ballantine, 2010.

Roosevelt, Eleanor. *Eleanor Roosevelt: In Her Words: On Women, Politics, Leadership, and Lessons from Life*. New York, NY: Black Dog & Leventhal, 2017.

Sherr, Lynn, ed. *Failure Is Impossible: Susan B. Anthony in Her Own Words*. New York: Crown, 2010.

Sider, Ronald J. *Just Politics: A Guide for Christian*

Engagement. Ada, MI: Brazos Press, 2012.

Thurman, Howard. *Howard Thurman: Essential Writings.* Ossining, NY: Orbis, 2006.

Tushnet, Mark V. and Randall Kennedy, eds. *Thurgood Marshall: His Speeches, Writings, Arguments, Opinions, and Reminiscences.* Chicago, IL: Chicago Review Press, 2011.

Tutu, Desmond. *God Has a Dream: A Vision of Hope for Our Time.* New York, NY: Image, 2003.

Walton, Mary. *A Woman's Crusade: Alice Paul and the Battle for the Ballot.* New York, NY: St. Martins, 2010.

Weise, Don, ed. *Time on Two Crosses: The Collected Writings of Bayard Rustin Kindle Edition.* Jersey City, NJ: Cleis Press, 2014.

Wells, Ida B. *The Light of Truth: Writings of an Anti-Lynching Crusader.* New York, NY: Penguin Classics, 2014.

Wiesel, Elie. *Open Heart.* New York, NY: Schocken, 2012.

Wilcox, Ella Wheeler. *The Heart of the New Thought.* Whitefish, MT: Kissinger Publishing, 2012.

Yousafzai, Malala. *I Am Malala: The Girl Who Stood Up for Education and Was Shot by the Taliban.* New York, NY: Little, Brown, 2013.

> Too frequently we think
> we have to do spectacular things.
> Yet if we remember that the sea is
> actually made up of drops of water
> and each drop counts, each one of
> us can do our little bit where we are.
> Those little bits can come together
> and almost overwhelm the world.
>
> —Desmond Tutu

Power and those in control concede nothing…without a demand. They never have and never will…. Each and every one of us must keep demanding, must keep fighting, must keep thundering, must keep plowing, must keep on keeping things struggling, must speak out and speak up until justice is served because where there is no justice there is no peace.

—Frederick Douglass

CONTRIBUTORS

Thank God that He has permitted us to live among the present problems. It is no longer permitted to anyone to be mediocre.

—Dorothy Day

Marjorie Bennet's first career was as a social worker, working with the urban homeless. "My experiences getting to know as individuals people who live their lives on the streets," she says, "changed me. It also contributed to the process of transforming me from a Christian into a Pagan. I went through a period of political activism—and then I became disillusioned. I decided the world could go to hell in a hand basket while I retreated to peaceful, green places where no one would bother me. As I immersed myself in the land and mythology of the Celts, however, what I had intended to be my escape proved to be what pushed me back to involvement with the outside world (and back to Jesus as well). I am not yet sure what form this will take during this part of my life, but I feel called to write, to use words and stories as best I can to speak out for tolerance and inclusion." Marjorie is working on a book, to be published by Anamchara Books, which is tentatively titled *The Celtic Faery-Faith: Confessions of a Pagan Follower of Jesus.*

Bruce Epperly is pastor and teacher at South Congregational Church, United Church of Christ, Centerville, Massachusetts, and professor in the areas of theology, ministry, and spirituality at Wesley Theological Seminary, Washington DC. He is the author of more than forty books, including *The Center Is Everywhere: Celtic Spirituality in the Postmodern World, Becoming Fire: Spiritual Practices for Global Christians, The Work of Christmas: The Twelve Days of Christmas with Howard Thurman,* and *The Mystic in You: Discovering a God-Filled World.*

A contemplative and scholar by orientation, he says, regarding his response to the call to justice, "I have discovered that pastoral ministry must have a prophetic dimension to be authentic in responding to the spiritual needs of our time. I see the calling of the mystic and spiritual leader as involving social transformation to enable persons not only to experience justice and equality but to enable rich and poor alike to have the ability to experience God's presence more fully. As a pastor, I am concerned that all have the 'leisure' to pursue their spiritual growth and that our nation's priorities ensure a world of beauty for generations to come." He is involved in environmental ministry and ministries with the homeless and vulnerable on Cape Cod where he lives.

Meg Llewellyn is the author of *Celtic Miracles and Wonders: Tales of the Ancient Saints*, as well as three adult coloring books in Anamchara Books' Contemplative Coloring series: *The Dragon in Your Heart, Celtic Bestiary,* and *The Tree of Life.*

She describes her response to the call to justice as being "stuttering but heartfelt," and goes on to say, "At this point in my life, I am struggling with how to find a central focus for my life that will include my love of Celtic history and mythology with the Divine demand I feel to be actively involved with building a better world. I daily feel the challenge to move from an academic fascination with the Celts to a lived experience of their values. For me this means, more than anything, that I find in Brigid a role model who shows me how to truly follow Jesus. She offers a template for the Christ-life that I find nowhere else in the modern Christian world. Her 'presence' in my life is an ongoing reminder to pay attention to others rather than live inside my own head. As an example, yesterday this meant that instead of driving by the man I often see with a sign reading, 'WILL WORK FOR FOOD,' I pulled over and talked to him. I found out that he is seventy-one and a retired construction worker, that his wife is dying of bone cancer, and that their Social Security payments don't stretch far enough to cover both the cost of her medications and the cost of food. I don't have Brigid's knack for creating endless butter, bacon, and ale, but I bought him a bag of groceries, and I plan to leave groceries on his porch weekly. When it comes to political involvement, I am still not certain what I am called to do—but I believe that what comes first, for me, must be having a 'Brigid heart' that's both sensitive enough to see where there is need and creative enough to formulate (and carry through with) a plan of action."

Kenneth McIntosh is the author of *Water from an Ancient Well: Celtic Spirituality for Modern Life*, *Magic Reversed* (a Celtic fantasy), *Celtic Nature Prayers: Prayers from an Ancient Well*, *The Green Man: An Ancient Symbol for the Modern World*, *Following Aslan: A Book of Devotions for Children*, as well as many young adult books, both fiction and nonfiction. He is also the editor of *The Winged Man: The Good News According to Matthew*, which is volume I in the Celtic Bible Commentary, as well as the author of several books in the Contemplative Coloring series, including *The Green Man* and *A Celtic Experience of the Book of Matthew*. With Lilly Weichberger, he is coauthor of *Brigid's Mantle: A Celtic Dialogue Between Pagan and Christian*. In addition to being an author, Ken is a teacher, speaker, and a pastor in the United Church of Christ.

In response to the question, "How do you respond to the Celtic call to justice," he says, "I see my role in life as being a mentor, and in that role I seek to give people the spiritual resources they need to work for justice long-term. Over the years I've seen activists turn bitter, angry, or, worst of all, just quit caring, because their inner resources are worn down. Teaching prayer and meditation practices, and the presence of God in the everyday, and the depths of the Scriptures on the topic of justice—all those are ways that I can equip activists with a strong inner center that will enable them to resist and persist."

Ellyn Sanna is the executive editor of Anamchara Books and the author of more than a hundred fiction and nonfiction books, including *All Shall Be Well: A Modern-Language Version of the Revelation of Julian of Norwich* and *The Thread,* a spiritual fantasy. Before devoting her professional time to creating books, she worked in a Mexican orphanage, in an inner-city crisis center, and as a teacher of students with special needs.

As the editor in chief of Harding House Publishing Service, she spent eleven years creating educational books for young adults. "Each of these books," she says, "offered young-adult readers opportunities to see beyond their own worlds, to catch a glimpse of other realities than their own. We created books focusing on the modern-day experiences of North

American indigenous tribes, on various forms of prejudice (whether against those with disabilities, those from other religious traditions, or those with skin of various shades), and on LGBTQ issues. My goal was always to open up readers' mental doors, even if only a crack, allowing new ideas to enter."

Today, through Daily Action (dailyaction.org), Ellyn makes phone calls and writes letters to her government representatives several times a week. However, she says that her activism is best represented by Dorothy Allison's words: "Writing is the only way I know to demand justice." Ellyn adds, "Each piece of writing has the power to change someone. Even if our words touch only a single person, that person will touch countless other lives. Writing and editing is how I contribute to the Realm of Heaven." She does this best, she says, when she pays attention, when she listens—and then gives a voice to those whose voices often go unheard. As the executive editor of Anamchara Books, she seeks to make Anamchara a bridge that can cross barriers and bring together spiritual traditions. She sees "Celtic spirituality" as a powerful model for the active affirmation of women, the "stranger," and the Earth.

Lilly Weichberger is a Celtic Shaman and Priestess. She teaches Celtic Shamanism, Magic, and Pagan spirituality, and has been a professional intuitive and reader for over twenty years. With Kenneth McIntosh, she is coauthor of *Brigid's Mantle: A Celtic Dialogue Between Pagan and Christian*. She also owns and runs Oran Mor, a small-batch artisan meadery in Roseburg, Oregon, which has become a local watering hole and safe space for all sorts of souls. She says, "Polarization is the plague if our times. As a Celtic Pagan, I am the child of centuries of resistance; as one of the posters in a recent women's march said, 'I am the daughter of the witches you failed to burn.' Resistance to tyranny is written in our Pagan heritage, and yet it is oh-so easy to fall into the trap of dualistic thinking—to demonize the 'other,' whether that other is an immigrant or a Democrat or a Republican. The 'othering' keeps us divided and at the mercy of those who benefit from fear and control. Our country is currently in the hands of those who feed on such fearfulness."

She goes on to say, "I moved from a liberal city to a small conservative town, and for the first three years here, I resisted—but not in a good way. I resisted owning my space here; I resisted being part of the community, unconsciously judging those around me as provincial and uneducated, ignorant, backwards, redneck—*other!* In my loneliness, I reached out again and again to my Gods, asking why I was here and when could I leave. Again and again, I was told my work was here.

"And then it happened, the kind of horror that always happens somewhere else, until it's your community: a mass shooting at a school I attended, a good friend and eight others dead, and any sense of safety I'd had shattered. For the first time, though, I saw the humanity of those around me rise up and shatter my preconceptions. Suddenly, I had strangers turning to me for solace and offering it in return. We formed connections that crossed all party and religious lines. We united in both our grief and our hope. We drew together in healthy resistance.

"Now my task in this community became clear— to create and hold a space where all are welcome in love, as long as they are respectful of one another. This idea sounds simple but it's truly revolutionary to this area. We have created a place where straights, gays, lesbians, transgender, nonbinary, tattooed folk, hippies, cowboys, rednecks, Pagans, and Christians all rub shoulders, sing together, drink together, cry together. I am a Celtic Pagan, while my business partner is a Trump-supporting Christian redneck. We are the most unlikely of partners, and there is much we don't agree on, but I watch day-by-day as the space he has helped me create rubs off on him and others like him. This is how I resist; this is how I answer my Gods' call to bring justice to the world. I know that my resistance is quiet in some ways compared to many others, but it is insidious and powerful nevertheless. It is a lived, practical, experiential resistance to hate, to othering, to the polarization that leaves us fearful and the puppets of madmen."

Finally, Lilly adds, "I may not be Christian but I have a great respect for Christ's actual teachings. When he said, 'Love thy neighbor as thyself,' he never put any limitations on that. And my Gods constantly remind me to see past fear and hatred to the Divine core of each person I meet, and to speak to that, to invoke that aspect of them, to resist the urge to other, so that bridges may be made to allow those in fear to cross over into another space, another potential, another vision of what can be, all with respect and inclusiveness. Do not mistake me, I do not agree with, nor condone the behavior of many people at this time in history, especially the insanity of what is happening in our government, and the racism, sexism, tyranny, bullying, and abuse it has engendered. These things must be resisted at all cost. Sometimes that is by marching and direct action, and sometimes it is by listening and providing a mirror that shows another way, by creating a safe space for marginalized and at-risk communities in an area where that support is rare and needed.

"And so I answer the call to justice by creating a safe haven in the most unexpected of places. To provide a living space of 'Namaste'—the Divine in me sees and honors the Divine in you . . . and calls it out, invokes it to manifest beyond fear, hatred, bigotry, and judgement. I do this in service of my Gods, no longer resisting their call, but surrendering to it, to live and love beyond illusion and human-created dualities. I resist now by living and loving fearlessly—and I intend to persist."

*It is in your hands
to create a better world
for all who live in it.*

—Nelson Mandela

www.ingramcontent.com/pod-product-compliance
Lightning Source LLC
Chambersburg PA
CBHW060514080526
44586CB00012B/478